A GARDENER'S
GUIDE TO

Cacti

Succulents and Foliage

Edited by Richard Rosenfeld
Series Editor: Graham Strong

MEREHURST

Merehurst Ltd, Ferry House, 51-57 Lacy Road, Putney, London SW15 1PR

CONTENTS

LEFT: *In this highly imaginative greenhouse display, the contrasting leaves, colours
and shapes of this group of cacti guarantee excellent year-round interest.*

GROWING CACTI

Although they are part of the large family of succulents, cacti are unlike any other group of plants. With distinguishing features such as ribbed surfaces, waxy coating and, of course, their spines, cacti deserve a special place in any creative display, invariably being grown in pots and used as focal points that are easily admired.

Cacti are magnificent plants giving architectural shapes of all kinds from tiny round balls to enormous tree-like growths, the kind of thing you see in cowboy films, and often superb flowers. In many cases the flowers only open at night, and can be wonderfully scented. Cacti need to be grown in pots, at least in winter, when the amount of drinking water they are given is strictly controlled. Too much is inevitably fatal. If they are not too heavy, pot-grown plants can be moved outside in summer, making the focal point in a bed of architectural plants. They can even be taken out of their pots, and placed in, for example, a special gravel bed, where there is excellent drainage. Alternatively, they can be grown in a special display bed in a large conservatory or greenhouse. Take care though not to confuse epiphytic cacti with the desert kind. The former tend to grow high up in trees, under the leafy canopy, in shady conditions. The latter demand day-long bright light.

KEY TO AT A GLANCE TABLES

PLANTING

FLOWERING

At a glance charts are your quick guide.
For full information, consult the accompanying text.

LEFT: A fine collection of well-grown cactus shows some of the extensive range of these fascinating plants. Variations in shapes and heights of the rounded barrel types with the vertical column cactus adds interest to the display.

GROWING CACTI

What is a cactus? What is a succulent?

A cactus is a succulent plant—but not all succulent plants are cacti. Succulent plants are xerophytes, plants able to escape or endure prolonged drought conditions. Succulents have the capacity to store water in swollen stems and roots, while some withdraw into the soil or shed their foliage in times of stress. Although succulent plants and cacti do share some characteristics, cacti have certain features that distinguish them from other plant families, including other forms of succulent plants.

FEATURES OF CACTI

Plant structure

Cacti are mainly round or cylindrical in shape, with a ribbed surface that allows for shrinkage as water is lost from the plant. The ribbed edges of cactus plants expose less surface area to the sun, which helps to reduce moisture loss. Waxy coatings on their outer surfaces also cut down moisture loss in extreme heat. Cacti have sharp, sometimes horny spines that deter animals from grazing and also provide some shade for the body of the plant. Cactus spines are in fact modified

GOLDEN BARREL CACTI dominate this carefully planned landscape of cactuses and succulents. These plants are growing in raised beds to ensure that they have perfect drainage.

leaves that have evolved to cut down moisture loss in the usually dry conditions of their native environment. There is a considerable range of spine types and sizes.

In cacti the breathing pores (stomates) enabling gas exchange between the plant and the atmosphere are located deep inside the plant walls and tend to be less numerous than those of many other plants. These stomates generally open only at night, avoiding water evaporation in the heat of the day. All cacti possess areoles, which are small woolly cushions from which emerge the spines and flower buds. These are found on top of warty protrusions known as tubercles. Many cacti have jointed parts that can be shed from the plant; these strike roots as they touch the ground and so aid in the distribution and continuity of the species.

Flowers

Cactus flowers are like jewels, glorious and showy, but they are also very short lived. Many last only one or two days while others are nocturnal, opening in the middle of the night and fading before dawn. The flowers have a silky or satiny texture and come in all colours except a true blue, although violet and purple are well represented. Many cacti have flowers in shades of pink, red or yellow. After the flowers have been pollinated, brightly coloured fruits form—these are usually red and very long lasting. In their native habitats, many cacti are pollinated by birds, especially humming-birds, while the night-flowering types are pollinated by moths, bats or other nocturnal creatures.

Types of cacti

Cacti are roughly grouped into three types: round or barrel cacti such as the golden barrel (*Echinocactus* species) and *Mammillaria* species; elongated cacti such as column cactus (*Cereus* species) and silver torch (*Cleistocactus* species); and jointed cacti such as *Opuntia* species and crab cactus (*Schlumbergera* species).

The cristate or crested cacti are the result of mutations that cause the growing tip of a shoot to broaden out into a band, forming strange, tortuous shapes. These mutations may be due to genetic changes or they may be due to the plant suffering unusual stress.

Native habitat

True cacti, almost without exception, are native to the Americas. Although not all cacti have their origins in real deserts, the greatest number of species occur in the low rainfall areas of the south-western United States and Mexico.

Cacti in these regions of desert plains endure scorching heat by day and often freezing nights. Sporadic rainfall of generally less than 25cm (10in) per annum allows the plants to store just enough water to survive. Heavy dews and the occasional snowfall augment the water supply. Snow insulates plants against cold and, when it melts, the water is directed to the plant roots.

The next largest group of species originates in the dry areas of central and eastern Brazil. Some cacti come from quite high elevations where conditions are still very harsh, but where the daytime temperatures do not reach the extremes of the true deserts.

On rocky slopes of mountains and high plateaux, the soil is often poor and the water drains away rapidly. Plants are exposed to intense sunlight and freezing night temperatures, high wind and often snow. Small cacti find a foothold among rocks and crevices that hold just enough water for survival while affording some shelter from wind. Many cacti from these habitats have dense woolly spines that provide protection from both searing sun and intense cold. Lower down the slope, large column cacti branching from heavy bases start to be seen. These and the large barrel types are able to withstand exposure to very strong winds.

A few species of cactus such as *Epiphyllum* and *Schlumbergera* are native to humid jungle environments where they grow as epiphytes on trees and sometimes on rocks. Although adapted to low light, they can also tolerate dry seasons. Some remain high in the tree canopy where there is more light while others start lower down, scrambling up as they grow towards the light.

Human use

A number of cacti have long been used by humans as food and in medicines. The fruit of some species is eaten fresh, cooked or dried. Indian fig (*Opuntia ficus-indica*) is probably the best known of these edible cacti, but the fruits of some of the hedgehog cacti (*Echinocereus* species) and the tiny fruits of some *Mammillaria* species are also considered delicacies. In Mexico, the aromatic fruits of *Ferocactus wislizenii* are stewed, candied and made into sweets, giving this species the common name of candy cactus. However, it is not recommended that you taste any part of a cactus unless you are certain that it is an Indian fig or another known edible variety. Many cacti contain alkaloids, which can be extremely damaging to health. On the other hand, heart-stimulant drugs are made from species of the cactus *Selenicereus*, which is widely cultivated both in the United States and Europe for this purpose.

Growing cacti under glass

It is very hard trying to group cacti with other plants; somehow they never look right. They are generally best arranged together, possibly with some excellent succulents. Fortunately, cacti come in such a wide range of shapes, from tiny quirky balls to grand theatrical vertical pillars, that you can always create a lively, contrasting mix.

The best displays of cacti are invariably in a large glasshouse where you can create a small scene from say South America. This gives you the space to plant the cacti reasonably well apart so that they can be seen from all angles, and with space to the front so that you are not endangered when they have got sharp, vicious spines. The cactus' shape is often so striking that its poor flowers seem unimportant.

Generally speaking, a dry environment must be provided, especially in winter, with bright light and excellent drainage. But when buying a cactus do try and find out where it comes from, so that you can provide the correct growing conditions. Unless you are very lucky, that almost certainly means growing them under glass, indoors or in a conservatory, where you can manufacture their special needs. And these needs mean either replicating desert or jungle conditions.

Established desert cacti grown in pots need three parts John Innes No. 2 with one part grit, well mixed together giving an open, free-draining soil. In summer they need watering (letting them dry out between each drink) and feeding as much as any thriving plant. Use special cactus feed or tomato fertiliser to encourage flowering. Over winter keep the plants dormant at about 7°C (45°F), only occasionally watering to prevent them from completely drying out and shrivelling. In fact over-watering is the commonest cause of death. When in doubt, do not water. Good light does though remain essential.

Strangely enough, some cacti prefer steamy, jungle-like conditions, which are harder to provide. Such cacti tend to be epiphytes which grow high in the branches of trees, not exposed in the open ground. You can still grow them in pots but you must provide a winter temperature nearly 10°C (50°F) higher than that for the desert kind, with year-round

A PROFUSION of clear yellow flowers conceals the whole top of this Trichocereus huascha (*previously called* Echinopsis).

TERRACOTTA POTS make ideal containers for growing cacti and succulents. Displayed at different levels, all plants can be easily seen.

humidity. The key to success remains open, free-draining compost, and in summer constant shade from strong sunlight (in the wild they would grow well protected by the tree canopy). A summer feed will boost the show of flowers.

Growing high up, these cacti tend to send out tumbling, trailing stems and they make good ingredients for a hanging basket. The Christmas cactus (see page 32) is an astonishing sight in full flower, especially when it is a flashy scarlet. Most people grow it as a pot plant on a table, and though fine, it is never as good a spectacle as when seen from below.

GROWING CACTI IN CONTAINERS

Cacti are easy-care potted plants and can be grown as single specimens or combined in shallow bowls to make a miniature cactus garden. Miniature cactus gardens can be of great interest. You could feature a mixture of several small-growing species or you may want to display a single fine, clustering plant that has been increasing over the years. Cacti are ideal for growing on balconies or patios as they do not mind drying out and appreciate shelter from the rain.

Cactus plants definitely look most attractive when grown in terracotta pots or glazed ceramic pots; in the glazed pot range, the ones decorated in blues and greens seem to suit the cactus best. When you are choosing a pot for an individual specimen, try to find one that is not much larger than the plant's rootball.

HANDLING A CACTUS USING FOLDED PAPER

WHEN HANDLING CACTI, use a band of cardboard or folded paper held firmly around the cactus to avoid the spines.

Cacti grown in containers must be potted into a very sharp-draining mix. For a small number of pots, it may be best to purchase a cactus mix from your local nursery. If you are potting a large number of plants or filling large pots, it will probably be more economical to buy the mix in bulk (if possible), or to buy the ingredients for making your own mix: this should include bags of special horticultural sand or grit (avoid builder's sand) and John Innes No. 2. Though you may think that desert cacti in particular grow in sand alone, that is not true. They need rather more soil than added drainage material. A ratio of three parts of soil to one of grit is fine.

Pots can be displayed on purpose-built stands, on pedestals or on the ground. Pots to be put on the ground should not be in direct contact with the soil and must be elevated very slightly to allow air to circulate under the pot base. You can purchase 'pot feet' or simply use pieces of broken terracotta or stone to elevate your pot.

Potted cacti team well with Mexican and Mediterranean style decor, for example, black wrought-iron furniture or rustic unpainted timber pieces. You could extend this decorating idea by adding some feature wall tiles.

Growing cacti outdoors in summer
Like most pot plants, cacti like to stand outside during the summer. Alternatively, they can be tapped out of the pot and planted in a special bed which is very free draining. This guarantees them excellent light levels while they are in full growth and ensures that they have plenty of fresh air. It also avoids the danger of baking in an inadequately ventilated or poorly shaded glasshouse. The chances of being attacked by greenhouse pests is also reduced. Overall, a spell outside gives healthier, sturdier plants.

What is more, creating a special group of cacti in a gravel garden which sets off their shapes, or on a rockery, adds style and interest to your garden. If you are growing the taller, column cacti try moving them outside before they become too big and then experiment with uplighting them at night. In a bare, minimalist garden they make quite an impact. It is absolutely essential to keep all spiny cacti well away from sites where children play.

HANDLING CACTI

To avoid injury from the spines when handling a cactus, use a band made of cardboard or folded newspaper. Place the band around the plant to steady it and hold firmly where the two pieces come together. This should prevent your hands from coming into contact with the spines and should not damage the cactus. You should, of course, also wear sturdy gloves. When handling larger specimens of cactus plants, you may need another person to help you. In this case, you should each use a paper band, or wooden or plastic tongs such as kitchen tongs, to lift and move the cactus. It is a difficult, heavy job to move large cactus plants but careful planning before planting—deciding on the new, permanent location of your cactus and preparing the planting hole—should help you to avoid problems in the future.

WATERING

It is important to remember that at any time of the year, cacti should only be watered when the soil or potting mix has dried out completely. Withholding water from plants may result in slower growth, but this is better than killing the plants through

RICHLY COLOURED SILKY FLOWERS on a cactus can look greatly at odds with the spines. In fact the flowers are often short-lived, though flowering reliably occurs each year. Two of the most reliable flowering kind are Rebutia and Mammillaria species.

watering too much or too often. Plants watered too often while they are dormant and unable to use or store water will rot and die. Large plants, because of their greater ability to store water, will need watering much less often than smaller plants. Potted plants will need watering more often than plants in the ground, especially during warmer weather, and the larger the container the less often it will need watering.

Until you feel confident about the frequency of watering needed, it is a good idea to dig into the soil or growing mix with a stick, a pencil or a thin bamboo stake to check the degree of dryness. In small pots, up to 10cm (4in) diameter, the top 2.5–5cm (1–2in) must be dry before more water is applied. In a 20cm (8in) pot, the soil should be dry at a depth of 7.5cm (3in) or more. Plants that have just been repotted should not be watered for at least a week afterwards. With any cactus, enough water should be applied at any one watering to thoroughly saturate the soil or mix. The frequency of watering will, of course, depend on the weather. If it is very hot and windy, plants will dry out much faster than they would in either warm, calm weather or cold conditions. In cold weather, plants may need watering only every 4–6 weeks or even less often, while in very hot weather they may need watering every few days.

Overhead watering will not hurt the cacti as it also washes dust off their surfaces, but do not do this late in the day, especially in humid districts, as water remaining on the plant overnight may predispose it to rotting. (You should note that some succulents should not be watered this way because of the waxy bloom on their foliage.) Alternatively, you should simply water the soil surface using a watering can or sit the whole pot in a container of water and allow the moisture to be drawn up from below. If available, rainwater is ideal for cacti. Cacti do not like alkaline water, so if your water supply is known to be alkaline, it may be worth collecting rainwater.

FEEDING

The most convenient method of feeding cacti is to use granular, slow-release fertilisers. A formulation containing trace elements, but low in nitrogen, is ideal. These fertilisers should be applied in spring to feed the plants slowly throughout their growing season. Follow the label directions and do not exceed the recommended amount. Feeding when plants are dormant may damage them and is a waste of fertiliser, which only starts to be released once soil temperatures rise. In the garden, you can use pelletted poultry manure as an alternative, but do not be too heavy handed.

PROPAGATION

Growing from seed

Seed is best sown in spring. Cactus seed should be sprinkled or placed on the surface of a seed-raising mix and lightly covered with the mix. You can mix very small seeds with fine sand for a more even sowing or put the seeds in a cone of paper from which you can gently shake them. Seed may germinate in a few days or a few weeks depending on the species. Keep the growing mix damp, but not soggy, by standing the pot in a container of water to draw up moisture, and then drain off any excess water from the seed-raising pot. Overhead watering will dislodge the seed. Once the seed has germinated, it may be several months before the seedlings are large enough to handle and pot up individually.

Although many home-grown cactus will not set viable seed because of the lack of suitable pollinators, it is possible to hand pollinate sometimes with good results. Use a small paintbrush to collect the pollen from one flower then gently

PROPAGATING BY CUTTINGS

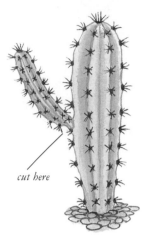

1. TAKE CACTUS cuttings by cleanly removing an offshoot from the parent plant.

cut here

2. THE BASE of the cutting should be slanted towards the central core of the stem. Dry the cutting for a few days before planting.

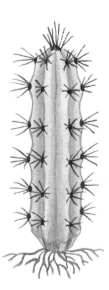

3. ROOTS are formed at the centre stem core. The amount of time taken to form roots varies with the species of cactus and the season of the year.

dust this into the centre of another flower. Pollen should go on to the stigma which is the organ in the centre of the flower surrounded by numerous pollen-bearing stamens.

It is fairly easy to collect seed from cacti with fleshy fruits. Once the fruit is fully coloured and ripe, pick off the fruit, slit open and squeeze out the seeds which should be cleaned and dried before sowing. It is more difficult to obtain the seed of cacti which normally shed their seed as the fruits dry and split. As the fruit is nearing maturity, a paper or mesh bag can be tied around the fruit to catch the seeds as they are dispersed from the maturing fruit.

Growing from cuttings

Some cacti form numerous offsets, which you can remove and pot up separately to start a new plant. Cut away any offsets from the parent plant by pushing a sharp knife down into the soil to sever any underground joints.

Some cacti can be propagated from cuttings of the plant, which must be taken with a very sharp, clean knife or secateurs. You should take cactus cuttings in spring, as the new growth begins. The cuttings or offsets with wounds must be allowed to dry for a few days, or a few weeks if necessary, until the cut area is completely dry and callused over. Cuttings can be taken from side shoots or even the head of the main stem. Slant the cut towards the core of the stem and allow the cutting to dry; this should encourage roots to develop from the stem core. When the cuttings have dried, insert them into very coarse sand. Plants should not be watered until roots start to form. The time that it takes for this to happen varies from one to six months.

Propagating by grafting

Grafting of cacti is usually done simply to produce unusual effects. Different coloured cacti may be joined together, or a barrel-shaped cactus may be grafted on the top of a column type. A flat graft is the easiest technique to use. Simply cut both the understock and the scion (the piece to be grafted on to the top of the understock) straight across, join the two sections neatly, and hold them in place with rubber bands or fine, strong cactus spines. At the optimum time of year— mid-spring to early autumn—the graft may 'take' within two weeks. Cleft and side grafts are also used, but these are not so easy for beginners.

BUYING A CACTUS

Many of the larger garden centres and nurseries will sell good-quality cactus plants that have been obtained from specialist growers. These are often small, reasonably priced plants, which will introduce you to the amazing range of cactus forms and become the beginning of a collection. Some specialist cactus nurseries sell direct to the public or by mail order. Garden centres and specialist growers are generally able to give you the right advice about the care and culture of your new plants. Novelty cactus are also on sale from florists or department stores, but the sales staff in these places are not, as a rule, qualified to give correct advice on cultivation.

Any cactus you buy must look clean and firm, and there must be no soft or decaying areas anywhere on the plant. It should not look pale or elongated, which would indicate that the cactus may have been kept for too long in poor light. The cactus must also be free of insect pests such as mealybugs, which resemble small, white, sticky patches of cotton wool and are often found between the spines.

WHAT CAN GO WRONG?

Cacti can be attacked by a range of sap-sucking insects such as aphids, mealybugs, scale insects, thrips and two-spotted mites. Healthy, vigorous plants grown in good conditions are much less likely to succumb to an attack of these pests.

If your plants are attacked—and if you cannot manually remove the pests—you may need to spray with a registered insecticide. You will sometimes be able to dislodge mealybugs and scale insects with a cotton bud dipped in methylated spirit. Overhead watering will often discourage mites and aphids.

Soft rots and root decay are almost impossible to treat if they have become well established. If this is the case, cut away the rotted section with a sharp, clean knife to expose any healthy tissue, remove a healthy section of the plant, and then dry it and treat it as a cutting. Dusting the exposed clean tissue of the cactus with sulphur is sometimes also helpful. Most rots are caused by overwatering, especially when plants are not in active growth. If you are unsure whether or not to water, do not! When you do water, soak the cactus thoroughly and then allow the soil to dry out before you water again.

GLASSHOUSE COLLECTIONS *offer a variety of shapes, like this magnificent vertical Euphorbia and Pandanus with pendulous leaves.*

PROPAGATING BY GRAFTING

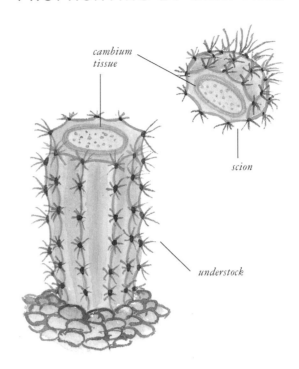

cambium tissue

scion

understock

1. WHEN GRAFTING, *is most important to line up the cambium tissue of both the understock and scion to ensure a good graft union.*

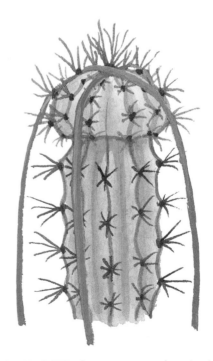

2. ONCE ALIGNED, *firm pressure must be maintained. Rubber bands can be used to go right around the graft and the pot, or use fine pins, cactus spines or toothpicks to hold the graft in place.*

APOROCACTUS
Rat's Tail Cactus

APOROCACTUS FLAGELLI *IS ONE of the most common types to be found and is quite easy to grow, it's colourful purple-red blooms adding a touch of vibrant colour to the garden in summer.*

FEATURES

Partial Shade

Aporocactus cacti come from Mexico and North America, and being epiphytic plants that grow high up in trees (as well as in rocky places), they are well worth growing in hanging baskets. They give an extremely good show of spring flowers, making a big bright display on top of the basket since they flower on the old growth, and not on the ends of the dangling stems, and generally provide very few problems. If the winter temperature falls much below 1°C (5°F) the flowering will tend to be later. And if the stems get too caught up (*aporos* is the Greek for tangled), removing the old ones after flowering prompts plenty of fresh new growth from the centre of the plant.

APOROCACTUS AT A GLANCE

Dramatic cactuses for a hanging basket, with long trailing stems and bright showy flowers. 6°C (43°F) min.

JAN	/	RECOMMENDED VARIETIES
FEB	/	*Aporocactus flagelliformis*
MAR	transplant	*A. martianus*
APR	repotting	
MAY	flowering	COMPANION PLANTS
JUN	flowering	Epiphyllum
JULY	/	Hatiora
AUG	/	Schlumbergera
SEPT	/	Selenicereus
OCT	/	
NOV	sow	
DEC	/	

Varieties — The two most commonly found plants are *Aporocactus flagelliformis* and *A. martianus*. The latter has larger flowers than the former. Appearing in early summer, they are vivid red on grey-green stems. The plant only grows to 12cm (5in) high, but can spread up to 1m (3ft). *A. flagelliformis* is easier to grow. Its hanging growth may reach 1.5m (5ft). Its purple-red blooms appear in spring when it makes a terrific sight with its snake-like stems topped by the colourful flowers.

CONDITIONS

Aspect — Being epiphytic, the plants need to be grown with some degree of shade during the day. It is particularly important during the hottest, brightest part of the day. A morning of sun, and afternoon of shade is fine.

Site — Grow in special epiphytic compost. Make sure that it is extremely free-draining.

GROWING METHOD

Propagation — Plants can be grown from seed sown in spring, but are easier to grow from stem cuttings taken in spring or summer.

Feeding — From late spring until late summer, provide a high potash or tomato feed once a month. Exceeding this dose is counter productive.

Problems — Will not thrive in full sun or if overwatered.

FLOWERING

Season — Rat's tail cactuses will flower either in late spring or early summer.

Fruits — Flowers are followed by papery fruits.

ASTROPHYTUM
Bishop's Cap

FASTEST GROWING *of all species of bishop's cap,* Astrophytum ornatum *bears many yellow flowers annually after about five years.*

DEEPLY DEFINED RIBS *and white scales around the upper body characterise* Astrophytum ornatum, *also known as star cactus.*

FEATURES

Sun

This very small genus originates in Texas and Mexico. The two most sought-after species are virtually spineless and covered in white scales instead. The bishop's cap or bishop's mitre, *Astrophytum myriostigma*, has an unusual dull purple, bluish or green body that is speckled all over with white scales. In the wild it may be 60cm (2ft) high and 20cm (8in) across, but in cultivation it is unlikely to reach melon size—and then only after many years. Its flowers are bright yellow, with the outer petals black tipped. *A. asterias*, known as the sea urchin or sand dollar cactus, is grey-green, slow growing and rarely more than 5–7.5cm (2–3in) high, eventually growing to a width of about 10cm (4in). It has spectacular bright yellow flowers with deep red centres.

ASTROPHYTUM AT A GLANCE

There are four species of these slow growing, attractive roundish cactuses that like arid conditions. 10°C (50°F) min.

		RECOMMENDED VARIETIES
JAN	/	*Astrophytum asterias*
FEB	/	*A. capricorne*
MAR	/	*A. myriostigma*
APR	sow ✍	*A. ornatum*
MAY	transplant ✍	
JUN	flowering ✿	
JULY	flowering ✿	COMPANION PLANTS
AUG	flowering ✿	Echinocactus
SEPT	/	Epostoa
OCT	/	Gymnocalycium
NOV	/	Mammillaria
DEC	/	Rebutia

Varieties   *A. ornatum* has pronounced spines on its very well-defined ribs. It is a cylindrical shape and it grows to about 30cm (1ft). During the summer it produces yellow flower. There are many different varieties and hybrids of these popular and attractive species. If you are just starting a collection of astrophytum, it is well worth growing *A. capricorne*, known as the goat's horn cactus. It is quite a small cactus, reaching a height of only about 25cm (8in). Its common name was inspired by the bizarre form of its twisted spines which wrap themselves around the cactus instead of sticking up vertically in the usual way. This makes handling the plant quite a problem as its spines tend to get snapped off very easily.

CONDITIONS

Aspect   Plants grow best in full sun, but may need a little shading if grown under glass.

Site   Soil must be very free draining and should contain very little organic matter.

GROWING METHOD

Propagation   Easy to raise from seed sown in spring.

Feeding   Give low-nitrogen liquid plant food in spring and mid-summer or use slow-release granules.

Problems   Overwatering causes them to rot and die.

FLOWERING

Season   Warm spring or summer flowering.

Fruits   Flowers followed by fleshy, ovoid green or red berries with long seeds within.

CEPHALOCEREUS SENILIS
Old Man Cactus

COARSE WHITE WHISKERY HAIRS *cover the whole of*
Cephalocereus senilis *but are more prolific on the new growth.*

GROUPED IN A RANGE *of sizes, these old man cactuses make a*
superb display with cotton ball cactuses in the background.

FEATURES

Sun

Possibly the best-known cactus of all, the old man cactus has wide appeal, and as a potted specimen, requires minimal attention. With its long white hair, it is just as interesting when young as when it reaches maturity. As a pot plant, it has the advantage of being rather slow growing and may only reach a height of about 30cm (1ft). In the open ground its growth rate is much faster. In the controlled climate of the glasshouse it can make a great feature. This column cactus can reach heights of up to 15m (50ft) in its native Mexico, but in cultivation rarely exceeds 1m (3ft). Its body is grey-green, up to about 30cm wide, and finely ribbed, but the detail of the ribbing is obscured by the long grey or white bristles. Pots need only be large enough to contain the root ball.

CEPHALOCEREUS AT A GLANCE

C. senilis is a marvellous cactus, with a beard at the top looking best on old plants. 5°C (41°F) min.

		COMPANION PLANTS
JAN	/	Cleistocactus
FEB	/	Echinocactus
MAR	repotting 🖐	Espostoa
APR	sow 🖐	Ferocactus
MAY	transplant 🖐	Gymnocalycium
JUN	flowering ✿	Mammillaria
JULY	flowering ✿	Parodia
AUG	/	Rebutia
SEPT	/	
OCT	/	
NOV	/	
DEC	/	

CONDITIONS

Aspect   To achieve the best results, grow in full, bright sun well away from any shade.

Site   Pot up plants in a mix of 3 parts standard cactus compost, plus 1 part limestone chippings. If being grown in a glasshouse bed, ensure that the soil is slightly alkaline.

GROWING METHOD

Propagation   This cactus is easily grown from seed sown in spring. Fruits split open when seed is ripe.

Feeding   Apply slow-release fertiliser in spring or feed monthly during the growing season with a low-nitrogen soluble liquid plant food.

Problems   No specific pest or disease problems are known if growing requirements are met. However, do keep a sharp look out for root mealybugs. The only other likely problem is caused by over watering. It is essential that you keep the compost completely dry over winter, when the plant is dormant. Any attempts to keep the soil wet will inevitably kill the plant.

FLOWERING

Season   The nocturnal flowers appear during summer, but plants grown indoors rarely flower and would need to be at least 20 years old to do so. Flowers are mostly pink, but may be cream. These blooms are evil smelling, no doubt to attract some night pollinator with a keen sense of smell.

Fruits   If pollinated, the flowers are followed by deep pink, fleshy fruits containing the seeds.

CEREUS
Column Cactus

THE LARGE AND VERY BEAUTIFUL *flowers of* Cereus uruguayanus *appear after dark and are worth waiting up for.*

THE BLUE-GREEN STEMS *of* Cereus *species are distinctly notched where the areoles and spines emerge.*

FEATURES

Sun

With a diverse range of origins from the West Indies to eastern South America, many of these cactuses are almost tree-like, while most form upright sturdy columns. The best-known species, *Cereus uruguayanus* (syn. *C. peruvianus*), is tree-like and can grow to 3m (10ft) or more with a stout, blue green body notched where spines emerge. The 'Monstrose' form makes a jumble of oddly shaped, blue-grey stems. Another tree-like species, *C. validus*, can also reach about 3m (10ft) high. Once established, it has pink-tinged white flowers in summer. *C. chalybaeus* is a column cactus, often tinged blue or purple, with well-defined ribs bearing spines that mature to black. Its flowers are also white with the outer petals magenta or red.

CEREUS AT A GLANCE

An excellent choice if you like tall, quick growing vertical cactuses, many with beautiful, night-opening flowers. 7°C (45°F) min.

JAN	/	
FEB	/	
MAR	sow	🖐
APR	transplant	✿
MAY	repotting	✿
JUN	flowering	✿
JULY	flowering	✿
AUG	/	
SEPT	flowering	✿
OCT	/	
NOV	/	
DEC	/	

RECOMMENDED VARIETIES

Cereus aethiops
C. chalybaeus
C. hildmannianus
C. uruguayanus
C. validus

COMPANION PLANTS

Astrophytum
Echinocactus
Gymnocalycium
Mammillaria

CONDITIONS

Aspect These cactuses prefer to be grown in an open situation in full sun. Keep them well away from even the lightest shade.

Site The soil must be free draining, but need not be rich. Column cactuses come from areas with poor rocky soil. Although the size and proportion of these plants make them easiest to accommodate in a desert garden, column cactuses can also be grown in containers, which may need some extra weight such as stones or gravel in the base to stop them tipping over. Note however that some, such as the columnar *C. validus* and *C. hildmannianus monstrose*, have the potential to reach 6m (20ft) and 5m (15ft). Of the two, the latter makes the most interesting shape with a contorted vertical stem.

GROWING METHOD

Propagation Grow plants from seed sown in spring or from cuttings of side branches.

Feeding Feed container-grown plants low-nitrogen liquid fertiliser monthly in summer. Ground-grown plants do not need feeding.

Problems Mealy bug and scale insects may cause problems.

FLOWERING

Season The large and lovely nocturnal flowers appear during spring and summer. The flowers usually appear after dark and fade before dawn.

Fruits Flowers are followed by round or oval fleshy fruits that ripen to yellow or red or purple.

CLEISTOCACTUS
Cleistocactus

TUBULAR FLOWERS grow directly from the stem of the silver torch cactus. A single flower near the crown creates a bird-like appearance.

BACK-LIT BY LOW SUN, the fine silvery spines of this cactus become a real feature as the silhouette of the narrow column is defined.

FEATURES

Sun

Although there are 45 species of *Cleistocactus*, all native to South America, very few are in general cultivation. Mostly branching from the base, these are upright column cactuses densely covered with fine spines that give them a silvery, woolly look. Although they look interesting as single stems, these cactuses are most spectacular when they are mass-planted. Their heights vary from 1–3m (3–10ft) but they are all fairly slender. The flowers, which emerge almost at right angles from the sides of the column, are mostly in shades of red and are pollinated by humming-birds in their natural habitats. The flowers never open very wide. These cactuses are fairly slow growing, making them ideal for pot culture, but they also can be grown in the open ground in conservatories. For plants in containers, regular potting on seems to produce the best growth.

CLEISTOCACTUS AT A GLANCE

These are generally quick-growing, spreading plants requiring plenty of space. Dramatic at full size. 7°C (45°F) min.

JAN	/	
FEB	/	
MAR	sow	
APR	/	
MAY	transplant	
JUN	flowering	
JULY	flowering	
AUG	flowering	
SEPT	/	
OCT	/	
NOV	/	
DEC	/	

RECOMMENDED VARIETIES
Cleistocactus brookei
C. hyalacanthus
C. jujuyensis
C. strausii
C. winteri

COMPANION PLANTS
Aeonium
Espostoa
Kalanchoe tomentosa
Ferocactus
Sansevieria trifasciata
Yucca

Varieties The most commonly cultivated species is *C. straussii*. It grows about 2m (6½ft) high and forms clumps almost as wide. It is the species most often known by the name silver torch, and has cerise-red flowers in summer. *C. hyalacanthus* (syn. *C. jujuyensis*) is usually less than 1m (3ft) high, with columns covered in hairy, brownish to cream spines and flowers that may be bright scarlet to orange-red. *C. brookei* has one of the biggest growth potentials. Its height and spread are indefinite. In the wild it forms a superb show of red or orange flowers.

CONDITIONS

Aspect The plants need a position with continuous bright light and frequent watering during the growing season when the summer is hot. Over winter they must be kept bone dry, with a severe reduction in water from late autumn.

Site Must have free-draining soil or cactus mix.

GROWING METHOD

Propagation Can be grown from seed or from stem cuttings or offsets during the warmer months.

Feeding Apply granular slow-release fertiliser in spring or feed the plants with weak solutions of liquid plant food through the growing season.

Problems Very susceptible to overwatering. If plants are indoors, mealybugs may be a problem.

FLOWERING

Season Flowers are red or pink, but also yellow, orange or green. Most flower in summer.

Fruits Small, rounded, yellow, green or red.

ECHINOCACTUS GRUSONII
Golden Barrel Cactus

PALE, STRAW-YELLOW SPINES smother the felted crown of the golden barrel cactus. Similarly, its ribs are fiercely spined.

A SPECTACULAR DISPLAY of golden barrels of varying size and age dominate this desert scene, enhanced by special mulch.

FEATURES

Sun

Although rare in its native Mexico, this very handsome large-growing cactus is in cultivation in many collections. It takes many years to reach its maximum size, which may be about 1m (3ft) wide and high. It does not flower until very mature and at least 40–60cm (16–24in) wide. Pot-grown specimens may possibly flower sooner than those grown in the open ground. The body of the plant is dark green and covered in long, fierce, golden yellow spines which produces a very decorative effect. Although most often known as golden barrel, it is also sometimes called mother-in-law's cushion. In time, it produces offsets to form large clumps, and is a most striking sight. This is not a difficult plant to cultivate, but you must have patience to see it reach its full potential.

ECHINOCACTUS AT A GLANCE

Marvellous cactuses which produce a ring of bright coloured flowers on top of the crown. 10°C (50°F) min.

JAN	/	RECOMMENDED VARIETIES
FEB	/	*Echinocactus grusonii*
MAR	sow	*E. horizonthalonius*
APR	/	*E. parryi*
MAY	transplant	*E. polycephalus*
JUN	flowering	*E. platyacanthus*
JULY	flowering	*E. texensis*
AUG	flowering	
SEPT	/	COMPANION PLANTS
OCT	/	Echinopsis
NOV	/	Gymnocalycium
DEC	/	Rebutia

CONDITIONS

Aspect Try to reproduce its natural habitat as far as possible by providing an open, sunny position. Do not retard development by placing it in the shade. Move it outside in its pot in summer.

Site Grow in a standard cactus mix of very coarse sand enriched with organic material. If you decide to plant it in the open ground for the summer months, provide plenty of added drainage material such as horticultural sharp sand or grit.

GROWING METHOD

Propagation This cactus can be grown from seed or by division of the offsets during spring or early summer.

Feeding Apply a weak liquid plant food every month throughout the growing season or apply granular slow-release fertiliser in the spring.

Problems This cactus may be vulnerable to attack by mealybugs, especially if it is grown in a glasshouse or a very sheltered situation. The threat of mealybugs is particularly likely when the plants are still small and young.

FLOWERING

Season Bright yellow flowers grow from the woolly crown of the plant in late spring or summer. This is one for the patient gardener as plants take a very long time to mature and flower.

Fruits The woolly fruits formed after flowering persist over a long period.
The flowers of plants grown in glasshouse conditions may need to be hand pollinated if the seed is to set.

ECHINOCEREUS

Hedgehog Cactus

CYCLAMEN-PINK *flowers stand like coronets to envelop the entire crown of this hedgehog cactus.*

PRETTY LAVENDER-PINK *flowers on* Echinocereus pectinatus *may be followed by edible fruits in ideal growing conditions.*

FEATURES

Sun

Hailing from the south-west of North America, all 47 species in this group are in cultivation. It is a very variable genus: some types are globular, while others form short columns, some of which are pencil thin.
The group is also split when it comes to their spines. Some species are heavily spined, while others are relatively smooth. Most are clump-forming or clustering, and in ideal conditions clumps of up to 1m (3ft) wide are found. Some species have edible fruits reputed to taste like strawberries. The best known of these are *Echinocereus pectinatus*, *E. engelmannii*, *E.reichenbachii* and *E. subinermis*. The range of flower colour in this group extends from white to yellow, orange, bright red, pale pink, magenta and violet.

ECHINOCEREUS AT A GLANCE

Dramatic small cactuses, with flowers bursting through the skin. Many attractive species. 10°C (50°F) min.

		RECOMMENDED VARIETIES
JAN	/	*Echinocereus chloranthus*
FEB	/	*E. cinerascens*
MAR	sow	*E. engelmannii*
APR	transplant	*E. knippelianus*
MAY	flowering	*E. pectinatus*
JUN	flowering	*E. reichenbachii*
JULY	/	*E. scheeri*
AUG	/	*E. subinermis*
SEPT	/	*E. triglochidiatus*
OCT	/	
NOV	/	
DEC	/	

Varieties *E. knippelianus* is a striking cactus, with a dark green, almost smooth body, few spines and pink to purple spring flowers. *E. subinermis* is one of the few yellow-flowered species, while *E. triglochidiatus* has brilliant scarlet flowers and a great range of forms. The 'must have' hedgehog cactus for any collector is *E. reichenbachii* with purple-pink flowers; it makes a tidy smallish shape being 30cm (1ft) high and 20cm (8in) wide.

CONDITIONS

Aspect Prefers full sun with good air circulation.

Site Use a well-drained standard cactus mix. If being planted outside over summer, dig plenty of grit into the soil.

GROWING METHOD

Propagation Can be grown from seed sown in spring or from offsets taken in spring or summer.

Feeding Apply slow-release granules in spring or use weak liquid plant food in the growing season.

Problems Outdoors, few problems are encountered. If plants are grown under glasss, mealybugs or scales may be troublesome.

FLOWERING

Season Flowers appear some time during spring or summer. The flower buds form inside the plant body and then burst through the skin near the stem tips, often leaving scars.

Fruits Flowers are followed by fleshy fruits, most of which ripen to red although some fruits are green or purple.

ECHINOPSIS
Echinopsis

A SCARLET-FLOWERED form of Echinopsis formosa *is one of the many free-flowering species in this group.*

A JUMBLE OF ODDLY SHAPED bodies of an Echinopsis *species illustrates the crested or monstrosa form of cactus.*

FEATURES

Sun

The botanical name of this group used to be *Lobivia*, an anagram of *Bolivia* where the largest number of species has its origins, although they also occur naturally in Peru, Chile and Argentina. Their habitats range from low desert country to dry high altitudes. There is a great range of shapes in the group, from low-growing globular to short cylindrical, and these cactuses generally have a clustering growth habit although a few are solitary. They are easy to grow and free flowering. The lovely flowers are produced from the side of the plant, lasting only one day as a rule. Some even flower at night. Flowers may be yellow, orange, red, pink or cerise.

ECHINOPSIS AT A GLANCE

Wonderfully varied group of cactuses, from small balls to tall columns, many with beautiful flowers. 7°C (45°F) min.

		RECOMMENDED VARIETIES
JAN	/	*Echinopsis backebergii*
FEB	/	*E. calochlora*
MAR	/	*E. candicans*
APR	sow	*E. eyriesii*
MAY	flowering	*E. huascha*
JUN	transplant	*E. oxygona*
JULY	flowering	*E. pentlandii*
AUG	flowering	*E. scopulicola*
SEPT	/	
OCT	/	
NOV	/	
DEC	/	

Varieties A popular species *Echinopsis backebergii* is variable both in form and flower colour according to the subspecies. Strongly spined and clustering, *E. pentlandii* has red, pink or yellow flowers. *E. huascha* is a cylindrical, fast grower that eventually forms a mound of congested stems with yellow or red flowers.

CONDITIONS

Aspect Grow these plants in full sun with good air circulation. Free air movement is especially important with clustering types that have many stems growing on top of one another.

Site Use a free-draining standard cactus mix. Outside, in the ground, ensure that there is plenty of added grit.

GROWING METHOD

Propagation Can be grown from seed or division of offsets in spring or early summer.

Feeding Apply slow-release granules in spring or feed with low-nitrogen liquid plant food about once a month through the growing season.

Problems This is generally a trouble-free group of plants if growing requirements are met. In fact echinopsis are remarkably robust, and can tolerate long periods of neglect.

FLOWERING

Season Flowers may appear in spring or summer depending on species and district.

Fruits The fruits of these cactuses are slightly hairy.

EPIPHYLLUM
Orchid Cactus

THE CENTRE of a lovely orchid cactus is dominated by a branched, star-like stigma surrounded by pollen-bearing stems.

EMERGING FROM the edge of the flattened stems, the rich red flowers of a hybrid orchid cactus cascade down from a basket.

FEATURES

Shade

Partial Shade

This group of epiphytic tropical American cactuses is known as orchid cactus because of the gorgeous, large flowers. Few of the true species are available, but the many spectacular named varieties have huge flowers 10–20cm (4–8in) across, in shades of cream, yellow, salmon, various pinks and reds. Some of these cultivars have a tendency to change colour according to light levels and temperatures. Stems of the orchid cactus are almost spineless, broad, flattened and leaf-like with flowers emerging from buds that are formed on the edges of these stems. These cactuses are natural epiphytes growing in tree canopies in tropical forests. As a result, they do well growing in hanging baskets or against a wall or tree that they can use for support as they scramble up.

EPIPHYLLUM AT A GLANCE

Stunning, beautiful often scented flowers on cactuses that look highly impressive in hanging baskets. 10°C (50°F) min.

		RECOMMENDED VARIETIES
JAN	/	*Epiphyllum crenatum*
FEB	/	
MAR	sow 👆	'Fantasy'
APR	transplant 👆	'Hollywood'
MAY	flowering ✿	'Jennifer Anne'
JUN	flowering ✿	*E. oxypetalum*
JULY	flowering ✿	*E. pumilum*
AUG	/	'Reward'
SEPT	/	
OCT	/	
NOV	/	
DEC	/	

Varieties   Some of the large-flowered types are slow to produce their first blooms and must be very mature before they flower regularly. However, the lovely species *Epiphyllum oxypetalum*, known as 'Belle de Nuit', is nocturnal with huge white, scented flowers unfolding on warm nights to close again by daybreak. If you only have room for one small orchid, *E. laui* is an excellent choice. It grows 30cm (1ft) high by 45cm (1½ft) wide, and produces scented white flowers about 15cm (6in) long.

CONDITIONS

Aspect   Unlike many cactuses, they prefer dappled, filtered shade out of direct sunlight.

Site   The soil mix must be relatively fertile, but above all open and free draining.

GROWING METHOD

Propagation   Can be grown from seed sown in spring, but hybrids must be increased from stem cuttings taken during summer to early autumn.

Feeding   Apply granular slow-release fertiliser in spring or regular liquid feeds in the growing season.

Problems   Usually trouble free in the right conditions.

FLOWERING

Season   Flowers are produced on mature plants from late spring through summer. Some flowers are quite long lasting. The original species are mostly night blooming, but the majority of those available today are day flowering.

Fruits   Red fruits may form on some plants.

ESPOSTOA
Cotton Ball Cactus

THE NEW GROWTH on this cactus is woollier than that of the mature growth. Spines protrude through the wool.

THE SCULPTURAL EFFECT of a cluster of columns of Espostoa lanata is an impressive feature in a dry garden.

FEATURES

Sun

This group has its origins in Peru, Bolivia or southern Ecuador and is currently undergoing a name change, with some botanists classifying it as *Facheiroa* species. These large, slow-growing, columnar cactuses may reach 3–4m (10–13ft) high, some branching from the base or higher up the column. Dense, white, woolly hair covers the column, almost obscuring its dark green surface. Flowers are generally nocturnal and form on tubular stems. Also known as snowball cactus, old lady or old man cactus, the species most often cultivated is *Espostoa lanata*, an impressive tree-like plant up to 4m (13ft) high. The main straight-ribbed trunk may be 20cm (8in) thick and can form a candelabra-like crown with numerous branches produced from the top of the plant.

Varieties — *E. melanostele* is shorter than some other species, rarely exceeding 2m (6½ft) in height. It may branch from the base in time. Its summer flowers are usually white, but can be yellow or brownish. A recent Brazilian discovery is *F. estevesii* which grows to 2m (6½ft) and has about 20 stems and pink flowers. It can only be seen in the wild.

CONDITIONS

Aspect — Grow plants in full sun or with a little light shade in very hot weather.

Site — Can be grown in almost any kind of soil as long as it is very free draining.

GROWING METHOD

Propagation — Grow plants from seed sown in spring or from cuttings taken in spring or early summer.

Feeding — Apply slow-release fertiliser granules in spring. Alternatively, apply a low-nitrogen liquid fertiliser every 4–6 weeks throughout the growing season.

Problems — No specific insect pests or diseases are known.

FLOWERING

Season — Flowers usually appear on the semi-mature plant in late spring or summer. Flowers of *E. lanata* are creamy-white, sometimes purple, and emerge from the side of the plant once it has reached a height of about 1m (3ft).

Fruits — After flowering fruits will appear. These can be either red or yellowish in colour. They are very fleshy.

FEROCACTUS
Barrel Cactus

THE FIERCE-LOOKING *red spines of* Ferocactus cylindraceus *are a very decorative feature of this plant.*

A MASS *of developing buds will ensure a long period of interest on this* F. echidne, *which is beginning to come into bloom.*

FEATURES

Sun

Named barrel cactus for their shape, these plants are also known as fish hook cactus because of the fiercely hooked spines on some species. Barrel cactus are generally large growers reaching 1–3m (3½–10ft) high and up to 30cm (1ft) thick in the wild, although some forms reach only 40cm (16in) at maturity. Most are solitary growers, but some form thick clumps after many years. These cactuses are easy to cultivate and grow quite rapidly. They can, however, be quite slow to reach their first flowering. Their shape is flatly spherical, and because of the colourful spines on top of the plant, barrel cactuses are often best viewed from above. *Ferocatus latispinus*, also called crow's claw, is popular for its reddish spines that lie flat on top of a compressed globe-shaped plant. Flowers are mostly pale purple, but can also be white or yellow in colour.

FEROCACTUS AT A GLANCE

An excellent beginner's cactus, many Ferocactus make superb shapely plants with bright, vivid flowers. 5°C (41°F) min.

JAN	/		
FEB	/		
MAR	sow 🖐	**RECOMMENDED VARIETIES**	
APR	transplant 🖐	*Ferocactus chrysacanthus*	
MAY	/	*F. cylindraceus*	
JUN	flowering ✿	*F. echidne*	
JULY	flowering ✿	*F. fordii*	
AUG	flowering ✿	*F. hamatacanthus*	
SEPT	/	*F. latispinus*	
OCT	/	*F. wislizenii*	
NOV	/		
DEC	/		

Other types   *F. fordii* grows to about 40cm (16in). It can bloom when it is still quite small, producing purple to magenta flowers. On the other hand *F. glaucescens*, which has a bluish-green body with yellow spines, must be very mature and perhaps 20cm (8in) wide before it produces its yellow flowers. *F. wislizenii* has very large, hooked spines up to 10cm (4in) long. It is known as candy cactus in its native Mexico, where its fruits are stewed and candied. There are about 35 species in total. Of them all, *F. fordii* is one of the easiest to buy.

CONDITIONS

Aspect   These are sun-loving plants, native to the arid regions of the south-western United States and Mexico.

Site   Soil must be very free draining, but should contain at least one-third organic matter. The standard potting compost is fine. Outdoors, the soil must be very free draining, with some added compost to provide moderate fertility.

GROWING METHOD

Propagation   Must be grown from seed sown in spring.

Feeding   Apply low-nitrogen liquid fertiliser about once a month during the growing season.

Problems   Generally a trouble-free group of cactus.

FLOWERING

Season   Large yellow, orange, red, white, pink or purple flowers appear in spring or summer. A sugary solution secreted in late summer attracts pollinating insects.

Fruits   Egg-shaped, fleshy fruits follow flowering.

GYMNOCALYCIUM
Gymnocalycium

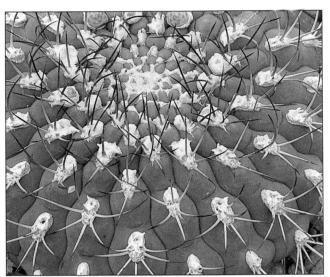

CLEARLY SPACED, woolly cushions or areoles from which the spines emerge are a feature of this excellent cactus.

A SOLITARY CHIN CACTUS growing in a steel blue ceramic bowl is set among a group of Haworthia *species.*

FEATURES

Partial Shade

This quite large group of cactuses originates in South America. Generally easy to cultivate, they make an excellent starting point for novice growers. Most of these plants are small and globular in shape, and may be either solitary or clustering in growth habit. They rarely exceed 10cm (4in) in height although there are some species that can reach 25cm (10in) or so. All have protruding spines. The largest species in the wild is *Gymnocalycium saglionis*, which can grow to 30cm (1ft) across. Its body is olive-green and the spines may be black, white or reddish brown.

Dwarf species Popular dwarf species include *G. andreae*, which bears yellow flowers in spring and produces plenty of offsets, and *G. bruchii*, which readily produces offsets to eventually form a low mat-like colony. Its flowers are pale pink and lightly scented.

Other types Flowering early in spring is *G. uruguayense*, with pale yellow to cream flowers displayed against the shiny green body. Its spines are bone coloured with a red base. There is another type of cactus in this group, known as spider cactus because the spines lie almost flat against the body of the plant in the shape of spiders. There are few of this type in cultivation, but the grey-green *G. denudatum* with its white summer flowers is a good example of the type. Probably the most dramatic kind is *G. mihanovichii* 'Red Head'. The top of the plant is red, and lacks any chlorophyll. It has been grafted on to a stock plant that supplies all its energy.

CONDITIONS

Aspect Plants prefer some shade, especially in summer. Give them morning sun only or grow them under 50 per cent filtered light.

Site Growing mix should be made up of about one-third grit and be very fast draining.

GROWING METHOD

Propagation These cactuses are easy to propagate in late winter or spring from seed, or by division of the offsets.

Feeding Apply liquid plant food monthly through the growing season or use slow-release granules.

Problems This is generally a trouble-free group to grow.

FLOWERING

Season Flowers appear in spring or summer and may be white, cream, yellow, pink or deep red.

Fruits The fruits that follow the flowers of chin cactus ripen a rich red.

GYMNOCALYCIUM AT A GLANCE

Highly attractive small rounded cactuses that like poor soil. Some produce marvellous vivid flowers. 5°C (41°F) min.

		RECOMMENDED VARIETIES
JAN	/	*Gymnocalycium andreae*
FEB	sow	*G. bruchii*
MAR	repotting	*G. denudatum*
APR	transplant	*G. horstii*
MAY	flowering	*G. mihanovichii* 'Red Head'
JUN	flowering	*G. saglionis*
JULY	flowering	*G. uruguayense*
AUG	/	
SEPT	/	
OCT	/	
NOV	/	
DEC	/	

Hatiora
Hatiora

BRIGHT ROSY PINK FLOWERS *of* Hatiora roasea *are produced in abundance in springtime.*

ALWAYS CHOOSE A CACTUS *with a striking architectural shape, and the flowers, even when they're as good as this, are a bonus.*

FEATURES

Partial Shade

These plants bear no apparent likeness to the spiny plants so readily recognised as cactuses. They tend to be upright in early stages, but become pendulous under their own weight and so are ideal for hanging baskets. A large potted plant may need heavy stones in the container base to counterbalance the cactus's weight. The stem segments are mid-green to bronze and are topped by small, yellow to orange tubular or funnel-shaped flowers in spring. This Brazilian group of plants includes ground growers and epiphytes and it is easy to imagine them growing from the fork or branch of a tree. *Hatiora salicornioides* is called drunkard's dream because the dense growth of tiny jointed stems resembles hundreds of tiny bottles. In Australia it is also called dancing bones.

HATIORA AT A GLANCE

Genus with many excellent species, well worth including in any collection of first-rate cactuses. 10°C (50°F) min.

JAN	/	
FEB	/	
MAR	sow	🖉
APR	transplant	🖉
MAY	flowering	✿
JUN	flowering	✿
JULY	/	
AUG	/	
SEPT	/	
OCT	/	
NOV	/	
DEC	/	

RECOMMENDED VARIETIES
Hatiora ephiphylloides
H. gaertneri
H. rosea
H. salicornioides

COMPANION PLANTS
Astrophyllum
Epiphyllum
Rebutia
Schlumbergera
Selenicereus

CONDITIONS

Aspect Drunkard's dream grows best in filtered sunlight or in a position that has morning sun and afternoon shade.

Site The epiphytic kind need some shade to replicate their natural growing conditions, just under the tree canopy. Either provide filtered sunlight, or a position with morning sun and reasonable afternoon shade. Spray regularly to provide high levels of humidity, especially on hot days, when in full growth from spring to autumn.

GROWING METHOD

Propagation These plants can be grown from seed sown in spring, but it is much easier to strike cuttings from the jointed stems in spring through to early autumn.

Feeding Apply a low-level nitrogen liquid feed once a month during the growing season.

Problems This is generally a very easy plant to grow and it has no specific pest or disease problems.

FLOWERING

Season Small, orange to yellow tubular flowers appear from the lower half of the plant in spring. Although the flowers are not spectacular, they give the impression of tiny lights on the ends of the stems. The most impressive thing about most of these plants, is their distinctive, unusual, non-cactus like dangling growth. From a distance *H. salicornioides* looks a bit like the jangled stems of a mistletoe.

Fruits The flowers of drunkard's dream are followed by tiny white fruits.

MAMMILLARIA
Mammillaria

THE MATURING RED FRUITS of Mammillaria prolifera surround each rounded stem. This species readily forms large colonies which makes it a satisfying plant to cultivate, both for the novice and more experienced growers.

FEATURES

Sun

This is probably the most popular group of cactus among growers and collectors and there are about 150 species in the genus. The largest number of these cactuses are native to Mexico, but their habitat also extends through the south-western United States south to Colombia and Venezuela. Instead of ribs, these cactuses all have tubercles which vary greatly in shape. These plants are sometimes also known as pincushion cactuses.

MAMMILLARIA AT A GLANCE

Some Mammillaria should be in every collection, for their flowers and shape, especially the terrific white snowballs. 7°C (45°F) min.

		RECOMMENDED VARIETIES
JAN	/	*Mammillaria baumii*
FEB	/	M. bocasana
MAR	sow	M. bombycina
APR	transplant	M. candida
MAY	flowering ✿	M. carmenae
JUN	flowering ✿	M. elongata
JULY	flowering ✿	M. geminispina
AUG	flowering ✿	M. hahniana
SEPT	flowering ✿	M. plumosa
OCT	/	M. zeilmanniana
NOV	/	
DEC	/	

Varieties While it is impossible to cater for all tastes, the following few species indicate the variety within the group. *Mammillaria carmenae* has feathery, white or cream spines fanning out from the woolly body, and rich creamy flowers. It rarely grows more than 10cm (4in) high, forming pretty clusters. *M. bombycina* has red, brown or yellow spines pushing through the woolly surface of the plant. This species is quick to make offsets to form a good-looking specimen, especially when topped with a ring of pretty cerise-pink flowers. *M. longimamma*, called the finger mound cactus, has fat, stubby tubercles like smooth, dark green fingers with tufts of yellow spines on each tip. Flowers borne in late spring are quite large and rich yellow, while fruits that follow are fleshy and green, not unlike the cactus itself. *M. geminispina* is another excellent cactus with small rounded shapes, and is distinguished by a covering of white spines, white areoles, and white flowers. Even better, after a few years it will start to produce plenty of young plants, eventually creating an eye-catching mound. Old lady or birthday cake cactus, *M. hahniana*, is named for the almost perfect ring of cerise flowers on the crown of the plant, which is followed by another ring of red candle-like fruits.

Snowballs *M. plumosa*, *M. bocasana* and *M. sempervivi* are so densely covered in white wool below the spines that they resemble snowballs or powder puffs—they are sometimes referred to by these common names.

THE SMALL CERISE FLOWERS of Mammillaria hahniana *encircle the crown of the plant when fully developed.*

THIS COLUMNAR SPECIES of Mammillaria *has its crown covered with buds and flowers in spring. It is very rewarding to grow.*

Growth habit Most of these cactuses are small and rounded and thickly covered with spines, but some have finger-like stems. Most produce offsets freely, making a good show in pots or in a bed, but a few, however, are solitary growers. These cactuses are popular and satisfying to grow not only because of their easy cultivation, but because they produce rings of beautiful flowers around the crown of the plant in spring to early summer even when quite young. Spines vary from straight to curved, soft and feathery to almost rigid, and come in variable colours.

Size There is a great variation in height and size, and although a few of these cactuses may reach 30–40cm (12–16in) in height, by far the greatest number will never exceed 15cm (6in). The ultimate spread of these species is harder to determine, but where there is space and where growing conditions are suitable, some may keep on spreading indefinitely. However, as it is easy to remove the offsets, their vigour need never be a problem.

CONDITIONS

Aspect Grow plants outdoors in full sun, but if they are under glass provide shading at the hottest time of day.

Site These cactuses are easy to grow. In pots, provide the standard cactus compost which will be free draining. When growing them in outdoor beds over summer, or in conservatory beds, make sure that the soil is on the poor side.

GROWING METHOD

Propagation These plants can be grown from seed sown in spring or by division of offsets in spring and summer. When the cactuses become quite prolific, as in the case of *M. geminispina*, it is worth removing smaller plantlets as they appear, not so much to create new plants as to maintain an aesthetically pleasing shape. It is also worth ensuring that one particularly good plant is always kept alone, without offspring, so its shape can be fully appreciated.

Feeding Apply small quantities of granular slow-release fertiliser in spring. You can also use low-nitrogen soluble liquid fertiliser at weak concentrations every month through the growing season.

Problems Some species form a thick tuberous root and these will rot if overwatered. *M. longimamma* is one of these, but all species must be considered vulnerable to overwatering.

FLOWERING

Season This cactus group produces its flowers during spring or summer, sometimes giving a second flush later in the season. They also tend to flower reliably year after year. The range of flower colours includes white, yellow and orange with a wide range of shades of pink, red and purple.

Fruits The berry-like fruits that follow the flowers are often bright red, but may also be green.

OPUNTIA
Opuntia

AN IMPENETRABLE BARRIER has been formed where two species of Opuntia *have become intermingled.*

FLAT, PADDLE-SHAPED segments and the sizeable growth of the edible Opuntia ficus-indica *make an impact in the landscape.*

FEATURES

Sun

Variously known as prickly pear, Indian fig and cholla, with many more local common names, this is a very large genus of cactus with a vast geographical range. Opuntia are jointed or segmented cactuses with mainly padded and flattened joints, although sometimes these are cylindrical or rounded. Species occur naturally from southern Canada and throughout the Americas, continuing to Patagonia on the tip of South America. Long grown as living fences in their native areas, many prickly pears were introduced to other countries for this purpose, with disastrous results.

Prickly pear *O. aurantiaca, O. stricta* and *O. vulgaris* and a number of other species have become quite appalling weeds in Australia, Africa and India. By 1925, there was estimated to be above 10 million acres (25 million hectares) of land infested by prickly pear in Australia. A huge programme of biological control was initiated, involving the introduction of the *Cactoblastis* moth and cochineal insects.

Indian fig The Indian fig, *O. ficus-indica*, is widely grown in many parts of the world for its fruit. It is a tree-like cactus up to 5m (17ft) high and wide.

Other types Although many species of opuntia are too large to place anywhere except in a large desert garden, there are numerous other shapes and sizes, with some that are suitable for pot culture. Bunny ears, *O. microdasys*, has dark green pads dotted with white areoles, and bristles that may be white, yellow or brown. The brown-bristled form is known as teddy bear ears. These plants rarely grow more than 40–60cm (16–24in) high and wide, and suit both containers or the garden. *O. tunicata* is a small, spreading bush about 60cm (24in) high and up to 1m (3ft) wide. Its thick, creamy spines take on a satin sheen in sunlight. Beaver tail, *O. basilaris*, has purple-grey flat pads with few spines and spreads by branching from the base, so is rarely more than 40cm (16in) high. *O. erinacea* is clump-forming with flattened blue-green pads, but it is the variety *ursina* with masses of fine hair-like spines—known as grizzly bear cactus—that attracts many growers. In the wild it grows around California and Arizona, has 10cm (4in) long pinky orange

OPUNTIA AT A GLANCE

The largest group of cactus with some outstanding plants; excellent shapes, flowers and dangerous spines. 5°C (41°F) min.

JAN	/	RECOMMENDED VARIETIES
FEB	/	*Opuntia basiliaris*
MAR	sow	*O. clavarioides*
APR	transplant	*O. ficus-indica*
MAY	flowering	*O. microdasys*
JUN	flowering	*O. imbricata*
JULY	flowering	*O. tunicata*
AUG	flowering	*O. verschaffeltii*
SEPT	flowering	*O. vestica*
OCT	/	
NOV	/	
DEC	/	

THE VIVID RED FLOWERS are tightly ridged across the top of the young leaves of this Opuntia. *The flowers of most species are usually produced in spring or summer, and are followed by succulent fruits later in the season.*

Chollas
flowers, and grows about 45cm (18in) high. It is well worth knowing something about this rare group, which are rarely seen outside specialist botanical collections. The chollas (pronounced 'choyas') are enormously variable in their habit of growth. They include the very spiny, almost furry-looking *O. bigelovii*, which grows to about 1–2m (3–6½ft) high, and the more open, tree-like *O. versicolor*, which may reach almost 4m (13ft) in height. Most of this group have easily detached segments, in particular the jumping cholla, *O. fulgida*, which hooks on to anything that passes, usually taking root and growing where it falls.

CONDITIONS

Aspect
Best grown in an open, sunny situation.

Site
Provide container-grown plants with sharply drained, standard cactus mix. In the garden, they tolerate a wide range of soils as long as they drain well. All opuntias dislike having their roots cramped in a small space. The larger plants should eventually be moved to a border in the glasshouse. If you opt for a regime of constant potting up, note that the spines are vicious.

GROWING METHOD

Propagation
Easily grown from stem segments which should be separated from the parent plant from spring to autumn. They can also be grown successfully from seed sown in spring.

Feeding
In spring and mid-summer, plants in the ground can be given pelletted poultry manure or granular slow-release fertiliser. Potted plants should have a dose of slow-release fertiliser in the spring or an occasional liquid feed during the growing season.

Problems
Few problems are encountered if growing conditions are suitable. The two worst offenders to look out for are scale insects and mealybugs. You will invariably need to spray to remove them, since the dangerous spines prevent you from getting in close to carry out treatment with a swab.

FLOWERING

Season
The flowers of opuntia are produced sometime during spring or summer, depending on species. The majority of species has yellow flowers, but these may also be orange, purple or white. For example, the bright yellow flowers of *O. tunicata* appear from spring to summer, while *O. basilaris* bears its bright rose-pink flowers in summer.

Fruits
Berry-like fruits form after the flowers fade, and in some species these are edible. The Indian fig has bright yellow flowers that are followed by deep red to purple fruit. It is widely cultivated around the world for its fruit. Prepare the fruit for eating by washing and using a brush to remove the spines. Slice off the top and bottom, slit the skin and peel. Serve in slices with a squeeze of lemon or lime juice. You can also use the pulp to make jam. *O. cochenillifera* is a source of cochineal—although today this dye is mainly synthesised.

PARODIA
Ball Cactus

DENSELY COVERED with fine yellow spines, the species Parodia claviceps *can be slow to form colonies.*

BRIGHT YELLOW FLOWERS are a feature of Parodia magnifica, *a deeply furrowed species which is not heavily spined.*

FEATURES

Sun

Partial Shade

While the species is now known as parodia, you will find that many ball cactuses are still under the old name of notocactus. These superb cactuses are native to Brazil, Paraguay, Uruguay and Argentina. Mostly rounded in form, although a few are column shaped, they are easy to grow and flower profusely. Many ball cactuses have deeply furrowed surfaces, but the coverage of spines varies greatly; some forms are thickly covered and others have quite sparse spines. *P. concinnus* is a small tubby shape with primrose-yellow flowers, while *P. leninghausii* can form a thick column up to 1m (3ft) high and has large yellow flowers. *P. herteri*, prized for its hot pink-purple flowers, is squat-shaped and blooms when it reaches tennis-ball size. *N. uebelmannianus* is another squat grower, with large purple or yellow flowers.

PARODIA AT A GLANCE

Parodia are generally globular or spherical, ribbed spiny cactuses from South America. Funnel-shaped blooms. 7°C (45°F) min.

		RECOMMENDED VARIETIES
JAN	/	*Parodia chrysacanthion*
FEB	/	*P. concinna*
MAR	transplant ✎	*P. herteri*
APR	flowering ✽	*P. horstii*
MAY	flowering ✽	*P. leninghausii*
JUN	flowering ✽	*P. magnifica*
JULY	flowering ✽	*P. mammulosa*
AUG	sow ✍	*P. nivosa*
SEPT	/	*P. rutilans*
OCT	/	*P. schwebsiana*
NOV	/	
DEC	/	

CONDITIONS

Aspect Ball cactuses will grow in full sun or in very light shade. When standing pots outdoors in summer, make sure that the plants receive some shade around midday.

Site When growing in pots, use a standard well-drained compost. In the ground, ball cactuses like equally well-drained soil with some well-rotted compost that slightly increases fertility.

GROWING METHOD

Propagation Grow from seed in spring or from offsets taken in summer. None of the species will produce offsets until quite mature. Increase watering in the spring and allow the soil to dry out between waterings during the summer.

Feeding Apply slow-release fertiliser in spring, or feed the plants with some low-nitrogen liquid fertiliser every 6–8 weeks throughout the growing season.

Problems This is generally a trouble-free type of cactus that is easy to grow.

FLOWERING

Season The flowers appear on the crown of ball cactuses during the spring or summer months. The central stigma of the flower is nearly always a deep reddish-purple to pink colour. While the majority of the ball cactuses have yellow flowers, it is possible to obtain other species that have attractive flowers in red, pink, purple or even orange colours. Contact a cactus nursery which specialises in parodia.

Fruits In ideal growing conditions, as in the wild, you may find that after the flowers fade fleshy fruits ripen to red.

PERESKIA ACULEATA
Barbados Gooseberry Cactus

THE BARBADOS GOOSEBERRY bears no resemblance to the traditional image of a cactus as seen in cowboy films. In the wild it makes quite a vigorous climber, spreading by means of flexible stems, and can grow 10m (30ft) high. In a pot it will be much more manageable.

FEATURES

Sun

Partial Shade

This most un-cactus-like plant starts life as a shrub, eventually becoming a vine capable of reaching a height of 8–10m (25–30ft). It is the only plant classified as a cactus that has true leaves. Native to the Caribbean and tropical regions of South America, the leafy cactus is cultivated for its edible fruit and is also known as Barbados gooseberry. The species forms robust, disease-resistant roots and is used as understocks on which to graft other cactuses. The Barbados cactus can be vigorous and spreads quite wide as well as climbing high. It has woody stems with strong, recurved spines which it uses to climb up a support.

PERESKIA AT A GLANCE

This is a remarkable cactus which should be in every specialist"s collection, but beware the vicious spines. 13°C (55°F).

JAN	/	**COMPANION PLANTS**
FEB	/	Aeonium
MAR	/	Aloe
APR	sow 👆	Cleistocactus
MAY	transplant 👆	Epostoa
JUN	/	*Kalanchoe tomentosa*
JULY	/	Ferocactus
AUG	/	*Pachypodium lamerei*
SEPT	flowering ✿	*Sansevieria trifasciata*
OCT	flowering ✿	Yucca
NOV	sow 👆	
DEC	/	

CONDITIONS

Aspect Grow in full sun or partial shade. Leaves stay green if given some shade at the hottest time of day; they can turn pinky yellow in full sun.

Site Soil must be well drained, but should contain plenty of organic matter. Re-pot annually and provide a stout, robust frame for the stems to climb up. This can either be a trellis which is firmly attached to the conservatory wall, or a series of taught horizontal wires attached to vine eye screws. The wires should be about 7.5cm (3in) away from the wall.

GROWING METHOD

Propagation Can be grown from seed sown in spring, but it is easier to strike from stem cuttings taken from spring to autumn.

Feeding Use pelletted poultry manure in a bed or slow-release granules in spring.

Problems Trouble free in the right conditions, but check against mealybugs and even aphids.

FLOWERING

Season Pretty white, cream or pink flowers appear in late summer or autumn. The flowers are lightly scented and can be quite long lasting. It only flowers in good conditions; guard against constant cool temperatures.

Fruits After flowering, fleshy yellow fruits form. These edible fruits have spines, which are normally easy to remove.

REBUTIA
Rebutia Cactus

THE LONG-TUBED YELLOW flowers stand clear of the cluster of crown cactus plants, allowing them to be fully enjoyed.

THE SMALL, ROUNDED BARREL shapes of Rebutia senilis *are entirely covered with fine spines. It has red and yellow flowering forms.*

FEATURES

Sun

This lovely group of cactuses flowers freely, regularly produces offsets and does not become very large. Occurring naturally in Bolivia and Argentina, often at high altitudes, these cactuses are round, barrel shaped or sometimes cylindrical, often with a very warty appearance but fairly soft spines. Flowers appear from the lower half of the plant. Many hybrids have been created, including a white-flowering form. *Rebutia krainziana* grows only about 5cm (2in) high, is densely ribbed and bears brilliant red flowers. *R. heliosa* has tiny button-like stems that eventually form a clustering mound with rosy pink flowers on top. *R. miniscula* (syn. *R. violaciflora*) rarely grows taller than 5cm (2in), multiplies freely and has bright cerise-purple flowers. Orange or yellow flowers are to be found on *R. fiebrigii* and *R. aureiflora*.

REBUTIA AT A GLANCE

These excellent South American cactuses flower early in the spring. Well worth creating a good collection. 5°C (41°F) min.

		RECOMMENDED VARIETIES
JAN	/	*Rebutia aureiflora*
FEB	/	*R. fiebrigii*
MAR	/	*R. heliosa*
APR	sow	*R. krainziana*
MAY	transplant	*R. guidols*
JUN	flowering	*R. pygmaea*
JULY	flowering	*R. senilis*
AUG	flowering	
SEPT	/	
OCT	/	
NOV	/	
DEC	/	

CONDITIONS

Aspect Full sun is absolutely essential, especially for a good spring display. Avoid any shade.

Site The growing medium whether in a pot, or in the ground outside over summer, must be moderately fertile and fast draining. Some can be kept at quite low temperatures over winter, just above freezing, if they are also kept dry.

GROWING METHOD

Propagation Many crown cactuses will self-seed but they are easy to grow from collected seed that is sown in spring or from offsets taken in spring or summer. Seedlings will often flower in the second year.

Feeding In spring, apply a small quantity of granular, slow-release fertiliser.

Problems This is generally a highly reliable, trouble-free group of cactuses. And the fact that some can withstand low winter temperatures, means that they are virtually indestructible. With the added bonus of bright, attractive flowers, they make a very good gift.

FLOWERING

Season Crown cactuses produce their flowers from mid-spring through summer depending on the species and district. The species have flower colours that include yellow, orange, pink, violet and red. A number of special hybrids have been created, including a form that has white flowers. *R. albiflora* is a rare white species.

Fruits Flowers are followed by small fruits that become papery as they mature, often releasing their seed around the plant.

SCHLUMBERGERA
Christmas Cactus

A VIVID SCARLET HYBRID of Schlumbergera truncata *makes a desirable potted plant to brighten winter days.*

FLOURISHING IN LIGHT SHADE, this Christmas cactus is the cerise-pink colour that most people associate with the species.

FEATURES

Partial Shade

This group of easily grown cacti originated from only about six species, and now features almost 200 cultivars of popular flowering pot plants which are more familiar to some as *Zygocactus. Schlumbergera* species, or Christmas cacti, are epiphytic and grow on trees or sometimes rocks in their native Brazilian habitat where their flowers are pollinated by humming-birds. Their popularity as pot plants is assured because most of them flower in autumn or winter, hence their common name. They have flat, jointed stems arching into small bushes, making them ideal for hanging baskets as well as pots. They come into vigorous growth in summer, and start flowering once the day length is less than 12 hours. Christmas cacti make excellent gifts.

SCHLUMBERGERA AT A GLANCE

High performance pot plants which give a big show of bright colour around Christmas. Easily grown. 7°C (45°F) min.

			RECOMMENDED VARIETIES
JAN	flowering	✿	*Schlumbergera 'Bristol Beauty'*
FEB	flowering	✿	*S.* x *buckleyi*
MAR	/		'Gold Charm'
APR	sow	🖐	'Joanne'
MAY	flowering	✿	'Lilac Beauty'
JUN	transplant	🖐	*S. opuntioides*
JULY	/		*S. truncata*
AUG	/		
SEPT	/		
OCT	/		
NOV	flowering	✿	
DEC	flowering	✿	

Varieties The silky, irregularly-shaped flowers are mainly in shades of pink or red, but hybrids can be almost pure white to cream, salmon, apricot, cerise, violet and scarlet. Some display yellow tones that revert to pink as temperatures fall. *S. truncata*, the crab cactus, and *S.* x *buckleyi*, the Christmas cactus, provide the origins of many of the modern hybrids.

CONDITIONS

Aspect Best in partial shade or with morning sun and afternoon shade in a sheltered situation.

Site For an established pot plant, John Innes No. 2 with added grit for good drainage is ideal. Repot every three years in the spring. It is too tender to be grown outdoors.

GROWING METHOD

Propagation These plants are easy to grow from cuttings of stem sections taken in spring or summer.

Feeding A light, regular summer feed will promote plenty of new growth and guarantee an excellent display of flowers.

Problems Generally easy to grow, these plants will suffer if grown in full sun and may not flower. Overwatering causes root rot and subsequent collapse of stems.

FLOWERING

Season Masses of flowers appear in autumn or winter. Once flower buds have formed, do not move the plants until buds begin to open. Flowers in spring if kept at 2–4°C (36–39°F) over winter. Gradually increase the temperature in spring.

SELENICEREUS
Selenicereus

THESE PLANTS ARE CULTIVATED for their beautiful white, cream or pale pink fragrant flowers, which open at night. It is amazing to see such a glorious flower emerge at dusk from a fairly ugly-looking stem but, of course, it will have faded by the following morning.

FEATURES

Partial Shade

There are about 20 species in this group of very long-stemmed climbing epiphytic cactuses. They are native to the forests of the south-western United States, central America, the West Indies and Colombia, where they live on trees or rocks. *Selenicereus* species have long been cultivated in Mexico for a drug used in the treatment of rheumatism and in Costa Rica for a heart-stimulant drug. They are now being cultivated in Germany and elsewhere for use in medicine, especially in the treatment of heart disorders. These plants have long, angled or tubular stems bearing small spines on the ribs, but it is their aerial roots that enable them to climb and cling on to their host plants. They will continue to grow upwards and spread as long as they find support.

SELENICEREUS AT A GLANCE

Strange, thin climbing stems with outstandingly beautiful, scented flowers, from South American forests. 15°C (59°F) min.

JAN	/	RECOMMENDED VARIETIES
FEB	/	*Selenicereus grandiflorus*
MAR	sow	*S. hamatus*
APR	/	*S. innesii*
MAY	transplant	*S. pteranthus*
JUN	flowering	*S. spinulosus*
JULY	flowering	
AUG	flowering	COMPANION PLANTS
SEPT	/	Epiphyllum
OCT	sow	Hatiora
NOV	/	Schlumbergera
DEC	/	Selenicereus

Varieties   *S. grandiflorus* is the species most often grown. Its flowers have outer petals that are yellow to brown, but the inner flower is pure white. Two other species found in cultivation are *S. pteranthus* and *S. spinulosus*. Both have cream, white or pale pink flowers. These plants can be grown in the ground, or rooted in large pots set against some strong support.

CONDITIONS

Aspect   Being epiphytic, these extraordinary cactuses need to be kept out of direct sunlight. They like filtered, dappled light, or as second best, light for half the day, shade for the rest.

Site   Plants need well-drained compost with added decayed organic matter. An orchid mix would suit them.

GROWING METHOD

Propagation   Plants are easily grown from stem segments taken from spring to early autumn. They can also be grown from seed sown in spring.

Feeding   Apply slow-release fertiliser in spring, or liquid feed occasionally in the growing season.

Problems   No specific pests or diseases are known, but keep an eye out in the summer for scale insects and mealybugs.

FLOWERING

Season   The spectacular, scented flowers do not appear until the plants have become quite mature. They open on summer evenings.

Fruits   The fleshy fruits are hairy or spiny.

GROWING SUCCULENT PLANTS

These unique plants vary greatly in size, shape and leaf colour, and they originate from a wide variety of habitats. One thing all succulents have in common, they are show-stoppers in the garden. They look striking against other plants, as contrasts or accents in the landscape, or when grown as individual eye-catchers.

A collection of succulents of different sizes and colours can make an attractive garden display without the need to add any other type of plant. They can also be used to vary and complement a display of cactuses to great effect. The other great advantage of succulents is that many of them can be teamed with a wide range of non-succulents without looking out of place. They can be used as feature plants, for your patio, and are also excellent for window box displays.

KEY TO AT A GLANCE TABLES

PLANTING

FLOWERING

At a glance charts are your quick guide.
For full information, consult the accompanying text.

LEFT: A perfect specimen of Agave *species dominates the planting in this well-planned succulent garden. The distinctive foliage of* Kalanchoe beharensis *fills the foreground while* K. fedtschenkoi *blooms in the background.*

FEATURES OF SUCCULENTS

Succulents are xerophytes, plants that store water in their stems, leaves or roots to withstand harsh, dry conditions. Their thick, fleshy leaves are often covered with a waxy coating or fine hairs to reduce loss of moisture through transpiration. Although some succulents have spines on their stems or foliage, these are carried singly and do not arise from areoles, the little 'cushions' that bear cactus spines. Succulents originate from a wide range of climatic regions.

Succulents come from a variety of habitats and while many are sensitive to cold, there are others that tolerate temperatures well below freezing. While all cactuses are in the one botanical family *Cactaceae*, succulents belong to a wide range of families that includes both the daisy family *Asteraceae* and the lily family *Liliaceae*.

SUCCULENTS IN THE GARDEN

Succulents are easy to incorporate into the garden as they mix very well with both cactuses and non-succulents, and they are particularly useful in the garden when planted to provide foliage contrast. Here, their distinctive forms and colours can be shown to great advantage. All that they require is to be associated with plants that enjoy the same aspect and have similar soil and water requirements.

The vast majority of succulents like to be grown in an open, sunny situation. The soil must drain well and if there is any chance of waterlogging, garden beds should be raised above the existing soil level as described in the introduction to cactus growing. The addition of some well-decayed compost or manure will improve soil aeration and drainage, as well as giving the plants a good start in life.

GRADED SIZES of terracotta bowls are used to display succulents. The top bowl contains Haworthia *species, the centre bowl has sedums and the lowest bowl is planted with echeverias.*

GROWING SUCCULENTS IN CONTAINERS

Succulents can be grown in almost any type of container as long as there is adequate drainage. They can be grown in standard pots or hanging baskets, troughs and window boxes, or turned into amusing novelties by planting them in old teapots or kettles, hiking boots, pottery ornaments or anything else that takes your fancy—as long as the container allows excess water to drain away.

Some succulents have enormous appeal for children, the most popular being *Kalanchoe tomentosa* and sedums. As long as the children do not kill these plants with kindness— usually by overwatering—succulents will survive with the minimum degree of attention.

The great range of colour in leaves alone can make for interesting groupings of pots of either single or mixed succulent species. A few succulents are also ideal for growing in hanging baskets. These include lampranthus and *Kalanchoe brossfeldiana*, while burro's tail must be grown this way. Mother-in-law's tongue, too, is most often grown as a container plant able to survive most conditions, both indoors and out. Large specimens of succulents can be used as feature or specimen plants in the garden or on a terrace. These include the Madagascar palm, silver jade plant, agaves and aloes. Those succulents that have sharp spines are best positioned away from regularly used paths and entrances. Succulents that rely on finely detailed foliage patterns to make their mark, such as *Agave victoriae-reginae*, make lovely potted plants positioned where their form and markings can be seen to best advantage. Slow growers such as this agave can remain happily in the one pot for many years.

A SURVIVOR of harsh conditions, this tender carpobrutus produces flowers on and off throughout the year in the wild.

WATERING AND FERTILISING

Most succulent plants prefer to be watered fairly regularly during the growing season, being kept drier during their dormant phase. Living in a very mild area with high winter rainfall need not rule you out of growing succulents, as long as the soil drainage is rapid. If your soil is sandy and quick draining, it will, of course, need watering much more frequently than a heavier and more moisture-retentive soil. As with all plants, you will need to become familiar with your own soil to gauge the frequency of watering required by succulents. However, succulents will generally not die rapidly if they run out of water, and it is better to water them too little than too much.

Most succulents can be grown without supplementary fertiliser unless the soil is extremely poor. Organic matter added to the soil before planting will often supply all the necessary nutrients, but low-nitrogen fertilisers can also be used during the growing season. Excess fertiliser, and especially excess nitrogen, will result in soft growth that may not stand up to tough growing conditions. If you feel that feeding is necessary, use granular slow-release fertilisers or half-strength soluble liquid plant foods. Small amounts of low-nitrogen fertilisers formulated to encourage flowering and fruiting, such as some tomato or rose foods, may also be suitable for some succulents.

PROPAGATION

Propagation from cuttings

Most succulents are very easy to grow from stem cuttings. If the stems are fairly slim, you can pot cuttings into coarse sand with a little added coir peat. Thick fleshy stems are best cut from the plant, dusted with sulphur and then allowed to dry for a few days before potting up. You can take cuttings from tips or from further down the stem—it does not seem to matter where the cutting comes from. The cuttings are best taken in the spring or mid-summer, when new roots will quickly appear. Most succulents will also grow readily from leaf cuttings. Simply break off a firm mature leaf cleanly,

PROPAGATING BY LEAF CUTTINGS

1. CLEANLY snap off a healthy, mature leaf from the stock plant and put it aside to dry.

2. INSERT only the leaf base into a mix of equal parts coarse sand and perlite, or coarse sand with a little coir peat.

3. NEW GROWTH emerges from the base of the old leaf. This may take a few weeks depending on the species and time of year.

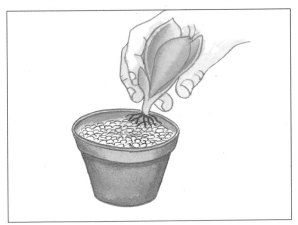

4. WHEN NEW plants are growing strongly and have good root systems, pot them on individually.

THE YELLOW-GREEN FOLIAGE of stonecrop Sedum nussbaumeranum *flushes pink in the sun. This is one of the 280 species of plants in the genus* Sedum, *many of which are good ornamentals. Their wide range of habitats varies from the tropics to cold regions.*

leave it to dry for a few days and then insert just the base of the leaf into the growing mix. One species which will root easily this way but never make a plant is senecio. The single leaves of this plant readily form roots, but never develop further. Some species will strike even if cuttings are left sitting on top of the mix, producing roots and tiny new leaves from the base of the old leaf. A few species develop bulbils on their flowering stems and can be detached and treated like cuttings to form separate plants.

Propagation by division

Some succulents form clumps in which individual plants have their own roots. In this case, simply dig up the whole clump and pull it apart, making sure each division has some roots and shoots. If, however, you have broken off a piece without roots, you should simply treat it as a cutting. Sometimes you will need to cut through the clump with a knife, which may result in the severing of sections of the plant. If you have cut through the entire plant, or even cut through half the plant, either discard that piece or dust it with sulphur before replanting it.

Clump-forming plants like echeverias or houseleeks are best propagated by division, but sometimes you may want to remove single rosettes to give to friends or, with the latter, grow them elsewhere in the garden. If you use a narrow-bladed knife or spatula, you can usually insert this carefully between rosettes to lever out individual plants.

Layering

Many succulents will produce roots wherever they come into contact with the soil. Once you know that a section has its own roots, it can be dug up and replanted. You can encourage this layering by pegging down a section of stem with a small stone, a hairpin or an opened paper clip. Good examples of these self-layering plants are lampranthus and London pride or *Crassula*.

Growing from seed

Although seedling plants may be slow growing and take a number of years to flower, many growers prefer this method of propagation as they find it very satisfying. If you want to try growing from seed, use a ready-made seed-raising mix or make your own from three parts of horticultural sand and one part of coir peat. Firm the mix into a container and water well. Sow fine seed on top of the mix and leave the container uncovered. Larger seeds can be covered to a depth of between equal to and twice the seed diameter. Use a spray mister to lightly water the seeds, cover the container with a sheet of glass or plastic and keep in a bright warm place, protecting it from direct sunlight. Check every few days to see whether the seed mix needs watering; if it does, use a spray mister or set the container in a larger one of water and allow the mix to slowly draw up the water from below. Do not water heavily from above as the water may dislodge the seeds that you have sown.

The time taken for seeds to germinate will vary enormously, ranging from a few days to several weeks. Once seed has germinated, leave the cover partially off the pot to reduce humidity without sending the tiny plants into shock. Increase this exposure to the atmosphere gradually until the seedlings are looking strong and the cover is entirely off. Once they are large enough to handle, they can be potted up into small, individual pots.

Unfortunately it is all too easy for seedlings to fail because of excess moisture in the potting mix and the atmosphere. Despite the high failure rate, it can be fun to grow succulents from seed. As the majority of succulents grow so easily from cuttings or division, not many growers bother to raise seeds. There are some species, however, that can only be propagated from seed. As with any other group of plants, there is always the chance that a seedling plant will exhibit some interesting variation in colour or form. These chance seedlings often give rise to new cultivars.

CLEAR YELLOW is one of the newer but quite stable colours among the hybrids of flaming Katy.

WHAT CAN GO WRONG?

Soil and watering
• Succulents are generally a very trouble-free group of plants. Their greatest enemy is heavy, poorly drained soil and an excess of water especially during the cooler months of the year. Most will take plenty of water during the growing season as long as the soil or potting mix drains well, but while the plants are dormant in cold weather, they will rot if the soil is kept wet all the time. A monthly watering would be adequate in a dry winter.

Pests
• Snails will sometimes eat some types of succulents leaving ugly scars that can ruin the appearance of the plant. Search for snails and destroy them or use a proprietary snail bait, taking care not to put pets or children at risk.
• Mealybugs can be a problem with any type of plant grown under shelter where conditions are dry and warm. These sap suckers, which resemble little sticky patches of cotton wool, can be wiped off with a cotton bud dipped in methylated spirits; if the infestation is severe, the plant may need spraying.

Weeds
• Weeds can spoil the appearance of a lovely patch of succulents but as many of these plants grow into clumps of rosettes or as low groundcovers, weeding can be difficult. It is hard to extract weeds without breaking these often brittle plants. Before you set your plants in the garden, turn the soil over well, water it and wait for weeds to appear. Remove the weeds by hand or spray with glyphosate. It is worth repeating the process if you have weed problems elsewhere in the garden. Make sure you dig out the bulbs of persistent perennial weeds, such as oxalis, prior to planting succulents. These stubborn weeds are almost impossible to remove completely if they appear amid a dense-growing cluster of succulents. Act before it is too late.

A STURDY COLUMN of fleshy leaves supports the pink flowers of this houseleek. This stem will slowly die off after the flowers fall.

AEONIUM
Aeonium

THIS SINGLE ROSETTE *of a variegated aeonium is just as decorative as the bowl of pansies behind it.*

THE BRANCHING HABIT *of* Aeonium arboreum *is seen in the dark mahogany cultivar 'Zwarkop', which is a worthy focal point.*

FEATURES

Sun

The flat, slightly glossy rosettes of succulent leaves are the common feature of this group of plants. Most are native to the Canary Islands, but a few are from other areas around the Mediterranean, notably parts of north Africa. Many make excellent tallish architectural pot plants which can enliven the summer garden. They also look extremely good by a pond where the reflection can be seen in the water. Flowers of most species are yellow, but can be white or pink. The most popular species in cultivation is *Aeonium arboreum*, with pale green rosettes 20cm (8in) wide on top of stems that may reach almost 1m (3ft) high. Its cultivar 'Zwartkop' has dark mahogany-red or deepest burgundy to purple foliage and will need maximum sunlight to maintain its colour.

AEONIUM AT A GLANCE	
Superb, often lean angular architectural succulents with rosettes of leaves on tall woody stems. Fast growing. 7°C (45°F) min.	

		RECOMMENDED VARIETIES
JAN	/	*Aeonium arboreum*
FEB	/	*A. a.* 'Zwartkop'
MAR	sow	*A. canariense*
APR	transplant	*A. haworthii*
MAY	repotting	*A. nobile*
JUN	flowering	*A. sedifolium*
JULY	/	*A. tabuliforme*
AUG	/	
SEPT	/	
OCT	/	
NOV	/	
DEC	/	

Varieties — *A. tabulaeforme* grows as a flat, single rosette around 35–50cm (14–20in) wide. In its natural habitat it grows on cliffs and must be protected from excessive rain, so that water never lodges in the crown. *A. haworthii* is more shrub-like, growing to about 50cm (20in) high. Its blue-green pointed leaves have a narrow red margin.

CONDITIONS

Aspect — Plants grow best in full sun all day with good air circulation. Avoid any shady situation, particularly with the near black 'Zwartkop'.

Site — Any fast-draining, gritty soil is suitable. Put a deepish layer of crocks at the bottom so that the water can quickly sluice away.

GROWING METHOD

Propagation — Can be easily grown from leaf cuttings or from individual rosettes during warm weather. Attempting to propagate from seed is very time consuming.

Feeding — Container-grown plants can be given a small quantity of slow-release fertiliser in spring.

Problems — Aeoniums should be trouble-free if growing conditions are correct. Avoid overwatering, especially in winter which can quickly kill the plant. In summer let the soil dry out between watering, in winter keep it dryish.

FLOWERING

Season — Species flower at different times. After a rosette has flowered, it will die off. It should then be removed to allow others to develop.

AGAVE
Agave

THE STRIKING, STRIPED foliage of the Agave americana *makes it a handsome plant worthy of a focal position.*

QUICK-GROWING AND SPINELESS, Agave attenuata *is safe to plant beside paths or steps. It can be grown in a pot or in the garden.*

FEATURES

Sun

There are few plants more striking than agaves. As garden features, their large rosettes of stiff leaves are a contrast for plants with softer or finer leaves. Their leaves generally have spiked margins and may grow to 1.5m (5ft) high. Flower spikes emerge from the centre of the plant and reach 3m (10ft) high in some species. Once an agave flowers, it will die, but by this time it will have produced offsets or suckers that continue to grow. Individual rosettes may grow over 1m (3ft) wide, and younger plants branch off from the base, eventually forming a massive clump. Agaves are native to the southern United States, Mexico and tropical South America. Many species are cultivated for the fibre in their leaves, while the sap of *Agave filifera* is fermented to make alcoholic *pulque* for mescal and tequila.

AGAVE AT A GLANCE

One of the great garden highlights is an architectural American agave in full flower. 5°C (41°F) min.

		RECOMMENDED VARIETIES
JAN	/	
FEB	/	*Agave americana*
MAR	sow 🖐	*A. americana* 'Mediopicta'
APR	/	*A. attenuata*
MAY	transplant 🖐	*A. filifera*
JUN	/	*A. parryi*
JULY	flowering ✿	*A. parviflora*
AUG	flowering ✿	*A. pumila*
SEPT	flowering ✿	*A. stricta*
OCT	/	
NOV	/	
DEC	/	

Varieties The century plant *A. americana*, was named because it supposedly took 100 years to flower. Actually, flowering occurs after 20–30 years. Spikes of creamy-yellow flowers can reach 6m (20ft) or more. The spined grey-green leaves can be 1.5m (5ft) long, recurving at the tips, and there are also striped forms. *A. victoriae-reginae* is handsome and compact with dark green leaves prettily patterned in white. Often growing only 50cm (20in) high and wide, this deserves to be featured in a pot.

CONDITIONS

Aspect Plants prefer full sun and an open site.

Site Agaves grow in most soils, even the slightly acid, but they must drain well. Average fertility is fine; it does not need to be high.

GROWING METHOD

Propagation Offsets can be separated from older plants during the growing season. Some will pull off cleanly, others need to be severed with a sharp knife. Seed, if available, is sown in spring.

Feeding On very poor soil, apply granular slow-release fertiliser in spring.

Problems This is generally a trouble-free group of plants.

FLOWERING

Season Some species of agave flower in summer, others in early autumn. Flowers can be cream, yellow or greenish in colour. In some species, these may not appear until the plant is at least 20 years old. The tall flower spikes can be amazingly dramatic.

ALOE
Aloe

THE FLESHY, TOOTHED LEAVES of Aloe vera *grow out in layers from the rosette centre. It is a clump-forming plant.*

A LARGE DESERT-STYLE GARDEN features tree-like species of Aloe, Yucca *and dry region palms.*

FEATURES

Sun

Aloes are often confused with agaves, but there are many differences, especially in flowering habit. Agaves flower only once and then only after very many years, but aloes produce their mostly red or yellow flowers each year once they are sufficiently mature. There are more than 300 species of aloes are native to tropical Africa, South Africa, Madagascar, the Arabian region and the Canary Islands. *Aloe vera* has been recognised for its medicinal and curative properties for hundreds of years.

A. vera This genus is probably best known by one species, *A. vera* (*A. barbadensis*), which is extensively used in shampoos, cosmetics and as a treatment for burns. The drug bitter aloes is derived from the juice of *A. ferox* and *A. vera*. *A. vera* is a clump-forming plant that suckers. It has thick, fleshy, grey-green leaves growing about 50cm (20in) high and yellow tubular flowers on a branched stem. This species is often container grown.

Other types The attractive *A. variegata* has dark green and white cross-banded foliage and coral-pink to bright red flowers. Growing to about 23cm (9in), this variegated aloe is also popular as a container plant. Another species with decorative foliage is *A. aristata*, which forms compact rosettes of dark green foliage spotted white with white-toothed margins. This is an ideal potted plant as it rarely grows more than 15cm (6in) high. *A. arborescens*, sometimes called the candelabra plant, may grow up to 3m (10ft) in height. Its many branches are topped with rosettes of leaves, and it has pinky orange flowers in winter. This is probably the species most often cultivated as an ornamental. The tree-like species known as fan aloe, *A. plicatilis*, grows to about 5m (17ft) and derives its name from the arrangement of its leaves on one plane, like a fan. Bright red flowers are held on stems well clear of the foliage. This species is dormant in summer and must have winter rain or irrigation. It is definitely one for the specialist.

ALOE AT A GLANCE

African, annual flowering succulents, many with striking strap-shaped leaves, and bright, vivid flowers. 7°C (45°F) min.

JAN	flowering ✿	**RECOMMENDED VARIETIES**
FEB	flowering ✿	*Aloe arborescens*
MAR	flowering ✿	*A. aristata*
APR	flowering ✿	*A. bakeri*
MAY	flowering ✿	*A. ferox*
JUN	/	*A. plicatilis*
JULY	/	*A. rauhii*
AUG	sow ✍	*A. variegata*
SEPT	/	*A. vera*
OCT	transplant ✍	
NOV	/	
DEC	/	

A SHRUBBY specimen of Aloe plicatilis *is already well branched despite being relatively young. It thrives in the reflected heat of a wall.*

IDEAL FOR CONTAINERS, Aloe vera *does not grow too large. Pots can be moved around to catch the sun.*

Growth habit Aloes can vary greatly in habit from those that are small, clump-forming rosettes to the single-stemmed or branching trees that may reach over 8m (26ft) in height. The stalkless leaves are succulent and mostly toothed, and they may be plain green or patterned. The tubular flowers of aloes are pollinated by birds in their native habitats. Flowering stems are sturdy and branching, which give a candelabra effect. They rarely, if ever, flower when grown indoors, but will tolerate quite poor growing conditions if given sufficient light. The strong sculptural form of the tree-like species can add height and great interest to a landscape of other lower-growing succulents. Two of the most outstanding are the orange flowering *A. africana* and the scarlet-orange *A. ferox*.

CONDITIONS

Aspect All aloes are best grown in full sun.

Site These plants must have good drainage in order to survive. The potting mix may need to have coarse sand or perlite added, to ensure that it remains open and free-draining, while garden beds will need to be raised above ground level if the soil is at all heavy. The top of a south-facing bank is often ideal, as is a specially prepared gravel garden which has excellent, fast drainage. The better the soil, the better the plants, the better the flowering.

GROWING METHOD

Propagation These succulents can be propagated from division of the offsets early in the season, from leaf or stem cuttings or from seed sown when ripe. Division of the rootstock produces the quickest results, since the new plants already have some roots. For speed of propagation, this method is followed by the taking of cuttings. Propagation from seeds is very slow and usually attempted only by the very patient.

Feeding Supplementary fertiliser is generally not needed by aloes. If you are growing plants in containers, however, or in very poor soil, they will benefit from slow-release granules applied at the beginning of the spring growing season.

Problems Aloes are generally easy to grow and trouble-free provided they are given free-draining soil and an open, sunny, frost-free site.

FLOWERING

Season Aloes flower and grow according to their southern-hemisphere biological clock. This means that in our hemisphere they will generally flower in the spring. One of the earliest to bloom is *A. candelabrum*, which comes into flower in early spring. Typically, aloes have clusters of small tubular flowers which are usually red, but they can also be striking combinations of orange-red, orange-yellow, red and yellow, etc.

CRASSULA
London Pride

PRETTY, STARRY FLOWERS lift the leathery looking foliage. Tiny plantlets often develop after the flowers have fallen.

ADAPTABLE AND TROUBLE-FREE, London pride can survive among rocks in tiny amounts of soil.

FEATURES

Sun

Partial Shade

In warm climates, this semi-prostrate plant is a very vigorous grower, but it can be useful and decorative as a groundcover or as a filler plant in a rockery. In any event, crassula is very easy to control if it ever exceeds its allotted space. It can be upright or somewhat sprawling in habit, and when sprawling it roots itself into the ground as it spreads. It can alternatively be grown in pots or hanging baskets. Plants grow about 15–25cm (6–10in) high, but can be taller. In warm, humid areas, one plant may spread 50cm (20in) or more in a season. The fleshy leaves may be rounded, oblong or spoon shaped, and the small pink and white starry flowers are carried on slender stems high above the foliage.

CRASSULA AT A GLANCE

Superb succulents with fleshy leaves ranging from the tiny to 5m (15ft) high in the wild. 5°C (41°F) min.

JAN	flowering ✽	
FEB	/	
MAR	sow ✍	
APR	transplant ✍	
MAY	flowering ✽	
JUN	flowering ✽	
JULY	flowering ✽	
AUG	/	
SEPT	flowering ✽	
OCT	/	
NOV	/	
DEC	flowering ✽	

RECOMMENDED VARIETIES
Crassula falcata
C. galanthea
C. helmsii
C. milfordiae
C. ovata
C. rupestris
C. sarcocaulis
C. schmidtii

CONDITIONS

Aspect   Crassula is suited to growing in sun or partial shade. Growth is more compact when the plant is situated in full sun. It benefits from being stood outside over summer, or it could be planted out in a special raised bed with excellent drainage.

Site   Almost any kind of well-drained soil will suit this plant. Plants in containers prefer a mix that drains well, but also contains plenty of organic matter.

GROWING METHOD

Propagation   This plant is very easily grown from stem cuttings taken any time during the warmer seasons. Tiny plantlets emerging from bulbils may sometimes form on the tips of flowered stems. These plantlets may be pegged down on a pot of coarse sandy mix to grow on and form roots.

Feeding   Potted plants may need some slow-release fertiliser applied in spring. Plants grown in beds rarely need supplementary feeding.

Problems   Crassula is generally an easily-grown, tough, trouble-free plant. The only problems occur in the glasshouse over summer, when you should keep an eye out for mealybugs and aphids and spray accordingly.

FLOWERING

Season   Small pink and white starry flowers appear in spring. These are sometimes followed by bulbils, which grow into new plants.

CRASSULA ARBORESCENS
Silver Jade Plant

ROUNDED SILVERY LEAVES edged in red make this shrubby succulent an asset in the mild garden, in or out of flower.

RUSTY RED-BROWN CALYCES remain on the bush long after the pale starry flowers have fallen.

FEATURES

Sun

Partial
Shade

Growing to over 2.5m (8½ft) in its native South Africa, this plant is more often seen at about 1.5m (5ft) when container-grown, or somewhat taller in the ground. It blends well with a range of plant types, including evergreens that enjoy the same conditions, and can be used most successfully to add height to a desert garden or a succulent display. It develops a sturdy trunk and numerous branches which carry leathery, grey-green oblong leaves with a fine red margin, sometimes dotted with tiny red spots. The popular *Crassula ovata* has smaller, green leaves.

CRASSULA AT A GLANCE

C. arborescens is a highly attractive South African succulent with pink autumn flowers and thick waxy leaves. 5°C (41°F) min.

		RECOMMENDED VARIETIES
JAN	/	*Crassula arborescens*
FEB	/	*C. falcata*
MAR	/	*C. galanthea*
APR	sow	*C. helmsii*
MAY	/	*C. milfordiae*
JUN	transplant	*C. ovata*
JULY	/	*C. rupestris*
AUG	/	*C. sarcocaulis*
SEPT	/	*C. schmidtii*
OCT	flowering ✽	
NOV	flowering ✽	
DEC	flowering ✽	

CONDITIONS

Aspect
Full sun is preferred, but this plant will tolerate shade for part of the day if necessary. However, the more light it receives the better it does.

Site
This plant can be grown in any type of well-drained soil. Container-grown plants will benefit from annual repotting, or from having the top third of the compost replaced.

GROWING METHOD

Propagation
This plant is most easily grown from leaf cuttings, which can simply be pulled from the stems. It can also be grown from stem cuttings or seed. All methods of propagation are best carried out in warm weather.

Feeding
Feeding is generally unnecessary, but a small amount of slow-release fertiliser can be given to container-grown plants in spring.

Problems
This is a tough, trouble-free plant that is quite easily grown. The only possible irritation is that the plant may repeatedly get too big for its container. Eventually, the best solution is to replace the oversize plant with a vigorous cutting. This will mean that you can start all over again with a small pot.

FLOWERING

Season
Flowering is profuse. Masses of small, pink, starry flowers adorn the shrub in late autumn to winter.

DUDLEYA
Dudleya

DUDLEYAS REALLY NEED to be grown under some form of shelter since the fantastic leaves can easily be mottled by raindrops. Group them round a cactus in a conservatory or to offset an aeonium. Alternatively, grow outside in summer.

FEATURES

Sun

Partial Shade

Dudleyas make striking pot plants and can be planted out over summer. They are very similar to echeverias, having rosettes of fleshy leaves, but these Californian and Mexican natives are often distinguished by their silvery white powdery covering. Take care when handling or watering because you can easily mark the 'powder'. There are about 40 species but only a handful are commercially available from small specialist nurseries. One of the best is the silver dollar plant *Dudleya brittonii* which can grow about 38cm (15in) high and 76cm (30in) wide. The leaves are strikingly white, and the pinkish flowers appear on top of stems which are from 50–90cm (20–36in) high. *D. pulverulenta* is about half the size but has red flowers. They are all relatively slow growing but form clumps which can be easily separated and grown on individually.

DUDLEYA AT A GLANCE

Interesting pot plants grown for their fleshy, tactile leaves and bright coloured flowers on long stems. 7°C (45°F).

		COMPANION PLANTS
JAN	/	
FEB	/	Aeonium
MAR	sow	Echeveria
APR	repotting	Haworthia
MAY	transplant	Kalanchoe
JUN	flowering	Lithops
JULY	flowering	Sedum
AUG	/	Sempervivum
SEPT	/	
OCT	/	
NOV	/	
DEC	/	

CONDITIONS

Aspect
Site
Grow in full sun or lightly filtered shade. Whether being grown in a pot or outside in the ground, the secret of success is excellent drainage. In the former use open, free-draining compost, and for the latter check that the soil has plenty of added grit and sharp sand. Continuous damp is fatal.

GROWING METHOD

Propagation
Though they can be grown from seed, this method is extremely time consuming. It is much quicker to slice off the new young plants that adjoin the parent with a sharp knife and pot them up over the summer. This method also results in a higher success rate. All mature plants should be kept dry over the winter when they are dormant.

Feeding
In summer provide a monthly feed. Since these plants are slow growing they do not need a continuous boost. In the garden, make sure that the soil is relatively fertile by applying a balanced fertiliser before planting.

Problems
Dudleya are prone to very few problems, but you must look out for mealybugs and treat accordingly. Be very careful when you are handling or watering the plants as it is very easy to mark the silvery 'powder' that enhances the leaves.

FLOWERING

Season
The tall vertical (sometimes prostrate) flower stems appear in the summer. They shoot up from the sides of the plant. The tubular, bell- or star-shaped flowers vary in colour. They can be pinkish, red or pale yellow.

ECHEVERIA
Echeveria

TIGHT, FORMAL ROSETTES of Echeveria elegans *take on reddish pink tones in cold conditions and full sun.*

VELVETY HAIRS COVER both foliage and stems of this attractive Echeveria setosa, *sometimes also called Mexican firecracker.*

FEATURES

Sun

Partial Shade

The formal rosettes of these plants were very popular for inclusion in Victorian (and later) bedding displays and are popular again now, often being used to fill decorative urns or shallow bowls to decorate a terrace or patio. They are ideal for sunny porches or verandahs as they will be protected from excess rain in that position. There is a huge range of shapes and sizes and even of foliage colour, and numerous hybrids have been developed. *Echeveria elegans* multiplies readily and can be grown in the ground or in a container. Yellow-tipped pink flowers on arching stems emerge from the rosette in spring. Like so many echeverias, after a few years the parent plant is surrounded and almost engulfed by its numerous offspring. They are easily removed.

ECHEVERIA AT A GLANCE

Mainly Mexican succulents offering fun shapes and flowers on tall stems. Use in summer borders. 7°C (45°F) min.

		RECOMMENDED VARIETIES
JAN	/	*Echeveria agavoides*
FEB	/	E. derenbergii
MAR	sow	E. elegans
APR	transplant	E. gibbiflora var. metalica
MAY	flowering	E. harmsii
JUN	flowering	'Perle von Nurnberg'
JULY	flowering	E. pulvinata
AUG	flowering	'Warfield Wonder'
SEPT	flowering	
OCT	flowering	
NOV	/	
DEC	/	

Varieties Both *E. pilosa* and *E. pulvinata* have leaves covered in soft hairs, giving them a velvety look and feel. These species form small, rather loose rosettes, which make less formal colonies than some of the waxier-looking types. Their flowers are yellow and orange to red. Some of the fancy varieties with red frilly edges on their leaves are known as painted ladies.

CONDITIONS

Aspect Most plants grow best in full sun, but a few species like a little shade.

Site Whether growing in the open ground or in a pot, ensure that the soil has plenty of added grit so that it is free draining.

GROWING METHOD

Propagation Most species are easily grown from division of rosettes. Some can be grown from leaf or stem cuttings taken during the warmer months. When dividing, slice off the attached baby plants when they are obviously growing quite well using a sharp knife, dip the end in rooting powder, and pot up. Initially keep well watered in light shade.

Feeding Lightly apply slow-release fertiliser in spring.

Problems Plants rot if they are too wet in cold weather.

FLOWERING

Season Bell-shaped, yellow, orange or red flowers appear at various times depending on the species, resulting in blooms in spring, summer and autumn.

EUPHORBIA CAPUT-MEDUSAE
Medusa's Head

CORONETS OF SMALL FLOWERS on the mature stems of
Medusa's head lighten the appearance of the heavy stems.

MEDUSA'S HEAD CAN BE PLANTED OUT over summer in a
gap between paving, producing a dramatic eye-catching effect.

FEATURES

Sun

Although growing only 30cm (1ft) high, this
multi-branched succulent makes an impact.
The rounded, thickened stem may grow partly
underground, but from this stout stem a mass
of grey-green knobbly branches emerge.
A well-grown plant may have a diameter of up
to 1m (3ft). Small green leaves sprout from the
tips of the warty branches. Ideal as a feature for
a desert or succulent garden, this plant can also
be container grown. Like all the plants in this
group, the milky latex in the stems is caustic
and may cause severe skin problems; wear
gloves and protect eyes when handling it.

EUPHORBIA AT A GLANCE

E. caput-medusae is a fine architectural South African plant with
branching stems and whitish flowers. 13°C (55°F) min.

		RECOMMENDED VARIETIES
JAN	/	Euphorbia amygdaloides var.
FEB	/	robbiae
MAR	sow	E. characias subsp. characias
APR	transplant	E. c. subsp. wulfenii
MAY	flowering	E. griffithii 'Dixter'
JUN	flowering	E. x martinii
JULY	flowering	E. myrsinites
AUG	/	E. palustris
SEPT	/	E. polychroma
OCT	/	E. schillingii
NOV	/	
DEC	/	

CONDITIONS

Aspect   These plants should be grown in full sun with
good air circulation around them.

Site   The soil must be well drained, but does not
need to be rich. Whether growing in pots, or
in the open ground over summer, make sure
that plenty of grit is added to the compost or
soil.

GROWING METHOD

Propagation   Medusa's head can be grown from stem
cuttings taken during the warmer months,
or from seed sown in spring.

Feeding   Plants grown in containers can be given a
small amount of slow-release fertiliser in
spring. Plants grown in the garden should
not need supplementary feeding. If the soil is
particularly poor though, a regular liquid feed
will give the plant a decent boost.

Problems   Medusa's head is generally not prone to
problems unless overwatered.

FLOWERING

Season   The cream or green flowers of this plant
appear in spring or summer. The true flower is
small, but it is fringed with attractive creamy
white, bract-like surrounds. In a poor summer
it may be best to move it back under glass
where it will flower better in the higher
temperatures.

EUPHORBIA MILII
Crown of Thorns

THE FLORAL DISPLAY of crown of thorns lasts many months but is more prolific in spring and summer.

THE WHITE-BRACTED FORM of crown of thorns is less vigorous than the species. It can be shaped into a neat and pretty pot plant.

FEATURES

Sun

This extremely spiny, semi-succulent plant sprawls over the ground. In warm-climate gardens it provides groundcover for places where people or animals are to be excluded, over walls or under windows, and is virtually maintenance-free. Heights vary from 1–1.5m (3 –4½ft) the latter in ideal conditions. It is valued for its almost year-round display of bright red bracts which surround the insignificant flowers. In a big pot it makes a very striking feature. The leaves are a soft mid-green and can be plentiful or sparse depending on conditions, warm and wet is best.

EUPHORBIA AT A GLANCE

An excellent if spiny plant, with good bright colours, demanding a warm, humid conservatory. 12°C (54°F) min.

		RECOMMENDED VARIETIES
JAN	/	*Euophorbia characias* subsp.
FEB	/	*wulfenii*
MAR	repotting	*E. dulcis* 'Chameleon'
APR	sow	*E. griffithii* 'Dixter'
MAY	flowering	*E. g.* 'Fireglow'
JUN	transplant	*E. x martinii*
JULY	flowering	*E. myrsinites*
AUG	/	*E. polychroma*
SEPT	/	*E. schillingii*
OCT	/	
NOV	/	
DEC	/	

CONDITIONS

Aspect
This has to be grown in a pot or border in the conservatory. Sun or light shade is fine. Note that the more you adhere to its ideal conditions, also keeping it warm and wet, the taller and bushier it grows, and the more frequently the flowers appear on new growth. In its native Madagascar it makes a highly effective hedging plant which keeps out all intruders. With limited room it may be best to keep it healthy without encouraging too much spiny growth.

Site
Grow in any type of soil that is free draining.

GROWING METHOD

Propagation
Propagate from stem cuttings taken in late spring or early summer. This is also a good time to prune the plant if you need to control its spread, and the prunings can be then used as a batch of cuttings.

Feeding
Slow-release fertiliser can be applied in spring, but this is unnecessary unless the soil is extremely poor.

Problems
This plant is generally quite trouble-free.

FLOWERING

Season
The long flowering period of this plant is technically from spring through to late summer. However, there are likely to be some flowers on it at almost any time of year in very warm conditions.

FENESTRARIA RHOPALOPHYLLA
Window Plant

THIS SOFT-LOOKING PLANT is sometimes aptly known as baby's toes. Foliage colour varies with growing conditions.

MATURE STEMS of the window plant are pale grey-brown with almost triangular windows of pale turquoise.

FEATURES

Sun

These curious-looking plants have upright, pale green leaves that look as if they have been sawn off because the flat surface on the top is a transparent window-like panel. The plant forms dense clusters of these stemless leaves, which may be up to 3cm (1¼in) long. In cultivation, all or most of the leaves can be seen, but in their desert habitat these are often buried in sand with only the 'window' visible. This window allows light to penetrate into the leaves. The burying of the stems is a protective mechanism that helps the plant survive the fierce sun of Namibia near the south-west cape of Africa. All but invisible, the plants are suddenly revealed when they burst into their bright yellow or white daisy-like flowers.

FENESTRARIA AT A GLANCE

F. rhopalophylla is a rarely seen plant for the glasshouse or summer garden, with bizarre, intriguing, tiny 'windows'. 7°C (45°F) min.

		COMPANION PLANTS
JAN	/	
FEB	/	Echeveria
MAR	transplant	Echinocereus
APR	sow	Haworthia
MAY	/	Kalanchoe
JUN	transplant	Lithops
JULY	/	Mammillaria
AUG	flowering	Rebutia
SEPT	flowering	Sedum
OCT	sow	
NOV	/	
DEC	/	

CONDITIONS

Aspect Window plants needs full sun all day. Keep them well away from any shady position.

Site Grow these plants in any kind of soil that is sharply drained or else plant them in gravelly sand. A surface mulch of small pebbles or pea gravel will help to reduce the humidity around the plant base. This surface layer will also help highlight the plant.

GROWING METHOD

Propagation These plants can be grown from offsets removed during warm weather, but the plants do not always transplant easily. Growing from seed is the most successful method, if sowings are made in autumn or spring.

Feeding Fertilising is generally unnecessary, but a small amount of slow-release fertiliser can be applied in the spring. When doing this take care not to be over zealous.

Problems Window plant is not difficult to grow as long as it is not overwatered. Excess water at any time, but especially in winter, will quickly cause the plant to rot.

FLOWERING

Season Flowering times may vary depending on the weather conditions and plant culture, but window plant generally flowers from late summer to autumn. *Fenestraria aurantiaca* has bright yellow flowers of the same size which appear at the end of summer and in early autumn.

Fruits A capsule-type fruit sets after flowers fade.

GASTERIA
Gasteria

GASTERIAS ALWAYS CATCH the eye with their prominent, stiff, outward- and upward-pointing leaves. They are remarkably easy to grow, and can stand outside over summer or planted in a bed, being brought under cover for the winter. Mature plants make excellent, large clumps.

FEATURES

Sun

Partial Shade

A southern African genus with about 16 species. The plants are shade-loving, drought-resistant perennial succulents with shallow roots. They are sometimes called ox tongues because of their long, stiff fleshy leaves which are mainly dark green with white spots or stripes. The leaves are always nearly paired opposite each other, but when mature the plants resemble rosettes. The tiny flowers appear along long, thin whippy stems and tend to be orange-red with green tips; to that extent they are very like echeverias. The young plants flower more in the spring, with older ones flowering longer through the summer and early autumn. While they can be stood outside over summer, in mid-autumn they will need to be brought inside because they do not tolerate the cold and wet.

GASTERIA AT A GLANCE

Striking showy leaves, best when heavily spotted, with a wonderful show of pale orange-red flowers. 7°C (45°F) min.

JAN	/	COMPANION PLANTS
FEB	/	Aeonium
MAR	sow	Agave
APR	/	Aloe
MAY	transplant	Echeveria
JUN	flowering	Haworthia
JULY	flowering	Kalanchoe
AUG	flowering	Lithops
SEPT	flowering	
OCT	/	
NOV	/	
DEC	/	

CONDITIONS

Aspect While they are perfectly happy in light, filtered shade, they will also tolerate bright sunny positions. Outside they can be used extremely successfully to front a Victorian-style bedding scheme, being arranged in symmetrical patterns.

Site The soil needs to be sharply drained. Add plenty of horticultural sand or grit to a summer bedding scheme before planting. In pots always make sure that you use open, free-draining soil.

GROWING METHOD

Propagation The quickest method is to remove offsets during the growing season, slicing them off with a sharp knife. Then dip the soft ends into rooting powder, and pot them up in a free-draining cuttings compost. This method is much quicker and more successful than growing by seed in the spring.

Feeding Outside, in the garden, one late spring application of a slow-release fertiliser is fine. Pot plants need a monthly low-nitrogen feed to keep them happy.

Problems Gasterias are remarkably trouble free and should not be afflicted by any particular problem.

FLOWERING

Season They flower in the spring when young, but older plants will provide a good show during the summer, possibly into early autumn. The small flowers make an open airy show, dangling from up to a dozen long thin stems. At this stage it is often worth bringing one or two plants inside and growing them on a windowsill for this unusual, impressive display.

HAWORTHIA
Haworthia

USED AS A FEATURE around a column cactus, dark rosettes of Haworthia *make a nice foliage contrast.*

ELONGATED ROSETTES of hard, fleshy leaves are a feature of several species of Haworthia. *Other species form tight, low mounds.*

FEATURES

Sun

Partial Shade

This fairly diverse group of succulents, native to South Africa, are generally undemanding and are popular with collectors as they exhibit so many variations. Many are stemless and all form clumps of rosettes. There is a great diversity of leaf shape and size, but many have white warty dots or tubercles on their surface including the pearl plant, *Haworthia pumila* (syn. *H. margaritifera*), which has leaves densely spotted with white on both surfaces, and *H. attenuata*, which has dark green fleshy leaves with a distinct line of white dots down the centre of both sides. *H. attenuata clariperla* is heavily spotted, the dots sometimes merging into lines. All of these form wide clumps in time, but rarely grow higher than 9cm (3½in).

HAWORTHIA AT A GLANCE

Highly distinctive South African succulents, the best with white dotted thick fleshy leaves. 5°C (41°F) min.

		RECOMMENDED VARIETIES
JAN	/	
FEB	/	*Haworthia attenuata*
MAR	/	*H. cymbiformis*
APR	sow 🖐	*H. fasciata*
MAY	flowering ✿	*H. maughanii*
JUN	transplant 🖐	*H. pumila*
JULY	flowering ✿	*H. reinwardtii*
AUG	flowering ✿	*H. retusa*
SEPT	flowering ✿	*H. tessellata*
OCT	/	
NOV	/	
DEC	/	

Varieties
H. truncata has fat, almost upright leaves that look like an irregular flight of small steps. *H. cymbiformis* is a soft-leaved species with translucent triangular leaves. It grows to 8cm (3in) high and has offsets forming a pretty clump. *H. reinwardtii* has upward-curving triangular leaves dotted with tubercles, forming a pillar about 15cm (6in) high. It forms an attractive clump in time.

CONDITIONS

Aspect
Some species take full sun, others prefer dappled sunlight or light shade.

Site
These plants must all be grown in a fast-draining, open sandy or gritty soil.

GROWING METHOD

Propagation
Easily grown from leaf cuttings or offsets taken in the warmer months. Alternatively, grow from seed sown in the spring but note this method is relatively time consuming. Cuttings are very much quicker.

Feeding
Normally grown without supplementary fertiliser, these plants can have a small amount of slow-release plant food as growth starts.

Problems
These plants are generally trouble-free if growing conditions are suitable. It is worth keeping a look out for mealybugs though.

FLOWERING

Season
Flowers, which are white or greenish, appear from spring to autumn according to species.

KALANCHOE BEHARENSIS
Feltbush

THE LARGE, WAVY LEAVES of feltbush are an uncommon colour and texture, making this plant a constant source of interest.

BRANCHED STEMS of small flowers stand well above the foliage on this old, established feltbush.

FEATURES

Sun

This is one of the many unusual plants native to Madagascar. Sometimes called elephant's ears or velvetbush, this tree-like species can grow to 3m (10ft) in height, but is mainly seen in cultivation at 1m (3ft) or so. The large leaves have wavy margins and vary in shape from almost triangular to arrow shaped; they can be up to 35cm (14in) long and are indeed felty in texture. The leaves are densely covered in bronze hairs that overlie the silver-grey or slightly olive base colour, and the undersides are quite silvery. In tropical-like regions, these plants are relatively fast growing, but may be slow growing in cooler conditions. Unlike any other plant, feltbush should be featured in a dry garden with other succulents or spiky foliage plants, or in a pot as a focal point.

KALANCHOE AT A GLANCE

K. beharensis is a bushy plant with attractive olive-green leaves that adds a distinctive touch to the border. 10°C (50°F) min.

		RECOMMENDED VARIETIES
JAN	/	*Kalanchoe blossfeldiana*
FEB	flowering ✿	*K. eriophylla*
MAR	flowering ✿	*K. grandiflora*
APR	flowering ✿	*K. marmorata*
MAY	repotting ✑	*K. pubescens*
JUN	/	'Tessa'
JULY	/	*K. tomentosa*
AUG	sow ✑	'Wendy'
SEPT	/	
OCT	transplant ✑	
NOV	/	
DEC	/	

CONDITIONS

Aspect This plant grows best where it has full sun for most of the day. If it is planted outside for the summer months it must have a sheltered site as it will not tolerate very strong winds. A sunny, south-facing position at the foot of a wall would be ideal.

Site Although the soil can be poor quality, it must be very fast draining. If growing these plants in a container, use standard potting mix but substitute one third of the volume of the mix with horticultural sand.

GROWING METHOD

Propagation Plantlets will form on the stems at the end of cut leaves in spring or summer. To propagate, carefully pull or cut off a leaf from the stem and plant it in a shady, humid place. Tiny plants should form after a few months. This is an extremely quick and highly efficient way of producing new plants. Though you can raise new plants by seed in the early spring, it is rarely worth the time and trouble.

Feeding Fertilising is not usually necessary, but a small amount of granular, slow-release fertiliser can be applied in spring.

Problems If grown in the right climate and not overwatered, feltbush is usually trouble free, with no known pest and disease problems.

FLOWERING

Season Feltbush produces tiny yellow-green flowers which may appear in late winter or spring on very mature plants.

KALANCHOE BLOSSFELDIANA
Flaming Katy

A MOUND OF BRIGHT RED FLOWERS all but obscures the foliage on this well-grown specimen of flaming Katy.

THREE VARIETIES of flaming Katy, bright pink, yellow and red, are used here as bedding plants with white alyssum.

FEATURES

Partial Shade

This is familiar to most people as a potted flowering plant. It has scalloped, fleshy dark green leaves, often edged with red, and the original species has bright scarlet flowers. It has been extensively hybridised and there are now forms with flowers in white, yellow and various shades of pink. There may be some colour change or variation depending on aspect and climatic conditions, especially as flowers start to fade. Some of the bright pinks tend to revert to the species scarlet. A very easy-care pot plant for use indoors or out, this is also a fine summer plant for the garden. In ideal warm conditions in the glasshouse border where there is plenty of space, the stems will sprawl and take root, creating new plants.

KALANCHOE AT A GLANCE

K. blossfeldiana is a superb, reliable pot plant with heads of bright flowers to brighten up the glasshouse. 10°C (50°F) min.

		RECOMMENDED VARIETIES
JAN	/	
FEB	flowering ✿	*K. beharensis*
MAR	flowering ✿	*K. eriophylla*
APR	flowering ✿	*K. grandiflora*
MAY	sow ✍	*K. marmorata*
JUN	/	*K. pubescens*
JULY	transplant ✍	*K. pumila*
AUG	/	'Tessa'
SEPT	/	*K. tomentosa*
OCT	/	'Wendy'
NOV	/	
DEC	/	

CONDITIONS

Aspect
In the garden, flaming Katy prefers morning sun and afternoon shade or light shade all day. Indoors, these plants should be given plenty of bright light.

Site
Flaming Katy grows best in a well-drained soil that also contains plenty of decayed organic matter. Planted in the shelter of a warm wall it will not get too wet in the summer.

GROWING METHOD

Propagation
Very easily grown from either leaf or stem cuttings, taken during the warmer months. The cuttings should be dried out for a few days before planting.

Feeding
In spring, apply slow-release fertiliser or a small amount of pelleted poultry manure in the open garden. It does not respond well to soil that is too fertile.

Problems
Flaming Katy is generally free of pests and disease.

FLOWERING

Season
The true flowering time is late winter to spring, but commercial growers now force plants so that they are available in flower almost all year round. In the home garden, in the ground or in pots, they should bloom at the proper time. Flowers will generally give several weeks of bright colour. After flowering, trim off spent flower heads.

KALANCHOE PUMILA
Kalanchoe

FROSTED WITH *a white sheen, the scalloped foliage of* Kalanchoe pumila *is attractive even without its pretty flowers.*

THE BLUE CERAMIC BOWL *makes a good foil for the generally silver foliage of this easy-to-grow plant.*

FEATURES

Partial Shade

This is a particularly attractive plant to grow in a container or hanging basket where it can be observed at close quarters. *Kalanchoe pumila* can also be shown to advantage at the front of a bed of mixed succulents or in a rockery. The silvery white bloom of its scalloped leaves is shown to advantage by a terracotta or glazed ceramic pot. In a pot, this plant tends to grow fairly upright, but in a basket its growth tends to become more pendulous. Bright cerise-pink flowers stand up above the foliage in spring. These plants rarely grow more than 20cm (8in) in height, but they continue to spread laterally. Once a clump is 30–40cm (12–16in) wide, the older growth in the centre may have started to die; repropagating and replanting will be necessary to renew it.

KALANCHOE AT A GLANCE

An excellent tidy plant, especially for hanging baskets, with pink flowers in the spring. 10°C (50°F) min.

		RECOMMENDED VARIETIES
JAN	/	*K. beharensis*
FEB	/	*K. blossfeldiana*
MAR	sow 👌	*K. eriophylla*
APR	transplant 🌱	*K. grandiflora*
MAY	flowering ❀	*K. marmorata*
JUN	/	*K. pubescens*
JULY	/	'Tessa'
AUG	/	*K. tomentosa*
SEPT	/	'Wendy'
OCT	/	
NOV	/	
DEC	/	

CONDITIONS

Aspect   These plants can be grown in either full sun or partial shade. If the position is too dark the production of pink flowers, about 1cm (½in) long, will be minimal.

Site   The soil or potting mix must be very well drained for these plants, preferably with some added organic matter. Keeping the roots in damp soil is highly detrimental, even fatal.

GROWING METHOD

Propagation   These plants are easily grown from either leaf or stem cuttings taken from spring to autumn. As the centre of the plant is likely to die when it reaches maturity, you should strike cuttings regularly if you wish to renew it. The best way to avoid a sudden desperate rush to propagate and keep this particular kalanchoe, is to take one cutting every two or three years. This should give you a good supply of plants, and if you ever find that you are over-stocked, give some away as presents.

Feeding   Container-grown plants should be given a little slow-release fertiliser in spring. In general, garden-grown plants do not need supplementary feeding.

Problems   This is generally an easy-care plant that is free from pest and disease problems. Look out for aphids and mealybugs though.

FLOWERING

Season   These plants usually carry small sprays of bright cerise-pink flowers above their foliage tips in spring.

KALANCHOE TOMENTOSA
Panda Plant

REDDISH-BROWN HAIRS *outline the tips of the leaves of the panda plant. Dense silvery hairs cover the rest of the leaf.*

BRANCHING STEMS *of velvety grey leaves make the panda plant very attractive. Both colour and texture make interesting contrast.*

FEATURES

Sun

The pale grey, felt-like or furry leaves of this plant have given rise to other common names such as pussy ears and plush plant. It is well suited to growing outdoors in gardens in the summer, but needs winter protection from the cold and wet. This is a plant with wide appeal for both adults and children. It just invites gentle stroking. The long oval leaves are slightly scalloped on their tips, which are marked a deep red-brown. Leaves are arranged in a kind of upright rosette and the whole plant has a bushy effect. In ideal conditions, it grows to almost 1m (3ft) high, but in cultivation to perhaps 40cm (16in). Flowers, which do not often appear on container-grown plants, are a greeny yellow bell shape with purplish edges.

KALANCHOE AT A GLANCE

K. tomentosa is a highly unusual Madagascan plant with marvellous soft furry leaves. A good present. 10°C (50°F) min.

		RECOMMENDED VARIETIES
JAN	/	
FEB	/	*K. beharensis*
MAR	sow	*K. blossfeldiana*
APR	transplant	*K. eriophylla*
MAY	flowering	*K. grandiflora*
JUN	flowering	*K. marmorata*
JULY	/	*K. pubescens*
AUG	/	*K. pumila*
SEPT	/	'Tessa'
OCT	/	'Wendy'
NOV	/	
DEC	/	

CONDITIONS

Aspect A position in full sun is essential for the best development and appearance of this species. There must also be plenty of good air circulation around the plant. When growing on a windowsill over winter, or in a glasshouse, be sure that it is not tucked away in the gloom.

Site The soil must be very well drained. Potting mixes for container-grown plants should contain a little organic matter. When growing outside over summer, dig plenty of horticultural grit into the soil.

GROWING METHOD

Propagation Break off leaves from the plant, dry them for a couple of days and then insert just the tip into very coarse sand. These should root readily in warm weather. Aerial roots sometimes appear on plants that are growing well. These sections can be removed and grown on separately during the warmer months.

Feeding A small amount of granular slow-release fertiliser can be applied in spring.

Problems As long as plants are not overwatered, there should be no problems.

FLOWERING

Season Flowers appear in spring on mature plants, but this does not always occur on container-grown plants except in ideal climates. Do not be put off by that though. The plant is only ever grown for its highly tactile, felty ears. The tiny flowers are virtually insignificant.

LAMPRANTHUS
Lampranthus

THE PROLIFIC FLOWERING lampranthus makes great seasonal impact. It is ideal as groundcover or for a border planting in dry areas.

A BRILLIANT TAPESTRY of colour is created in this mixed planting which highlights the use of lampranthus.

FEATURES

Sun

This group of plants is native to South Africa and is ideal for low-maintenance gardens in areas with low rainfall. Lampranthus is best known as a creeping or trailing plant used as a groundcover, but some species are bushier and more like shrubs. Stems of many species root as they spread, making them ideal for soil binding on banks in frost free areas. The fleshy grey-green leaves are angled or cylindrical, and growing stems may reach 50cm (20in) or so, but are more often around 30cm (12in). Individual plants may spread 30cm (12in) or more in a growing season. The daisy-like flowers, which only open in sun, are shiny, brilliantly coloured and borne in such profusion that the foliage and stems are all but obscured.

LAMPRANTHUS AT A GLANCE

Prime ingredients for a dry seaside summer garden, offering big bright clusters of flowers. 7°C (45°F) min.

			RECOMMENDED VARIETIES
JAN	/		*Lampranthus aurantiacus*
FEB	flowering	❀	*L. aureus*
MAR	sow	☞	*L. brownii*
APR	/		*L. haworthii*
MAY	/		*L. spectabilis*
JUN	transplant	☞	*L. s.* 'Tresco Brilliant'
JULY	flowering	❀	
AUG	flowering	❀	
SEPT	flowering	❀	
OCT	/		
NOV	/		
DEC	/		

Varieties   Species commonly grown include *Lampranthus aurantiacus*, with orange flowers; *L. roseus*, with pink flowers; and *L. spectabilis*, with purple to magenta flowers. Many lampranthus sold in nurseries are cultivars or hybrids bred for garden use.

CONDITIONS

Aspect   These plants must be grown in full sun or flowers will not open.

Site   Can be grown in almost any type of soil as long as it is well drained. Try to replicate its natural habitat which is mainly coastal South African near-desert conditions; dry and arid.

GROWING METHOD

Propagation   Lampranthus are easily grown from stem cuttings taken from spring to autumn. Species can be grown from seed sown in spring.

Feeding   Fertilising is generally unnecessary as plants grown 'hard' usually flower better.

Problems   Snails sometimes graze on foliage causing damage. Plants will not survive in heavy, poorly drained soil.

FLOWERING

Season   Flowers appear through late winter and spring or during summer depending on the conditions and the species grown. Flowers may be orange, red, yellow, purple, cream and many shades in between. In good conditions they will provide excellent, striking colours, especially the bright orange *L. aurantiacus*.

LEWISIA
Lewesia

LEWISIAS ARE SMALL, highly attractive plants that thrive, and really stand out, in a gravel garden or on a sunny slope. They should always be grouped together for maximum impact. The result is a good show of flowers in the spring and early summer.

FEATURES

Sun

The genus has 19 or 20 hardy species, and is exclusively American. The best place to grow them is on a well-drained south-facing slope, in a rock garden or even on a wall. They are low growing, often with bright flowers which are funnel shaped. The colour range is mainly on the pink-magenta side, with some that are yellow and white. There are many excellent kinds to chose from, the best being *L. bracyhcalyx* which flowers in late spring and early summer, *L. cotyledon* which flowers from spring to summer in purple-pink, and *L. tweedyi* which flowers at the same time in a peachy-pink colour. The best thing about lewisias is that they hybridise easily, and a collection of different plants should soon yield interesting offspring. The excellent Cotyledon Hybrids come in all colours from yellow-orange to magenta.

LEWISIA AT A GLANCE

Marvellous small early season flowers in a wide range of colours. Excellent in small pots. Hardy to -15°C (5°F).

		RECOMMENDED VARIETIES
JAN	/	*Lewisia brachycalyx*
FEB	/	*L. cotyledon*
MAR	repotting 🖐	*L. c. Sunset Group*
APR	/	*L. Cotyledon Hybrids*
MAY	flowering ✽	'De Pauley'
JUN	flowering ✽	'George Henley'
JULY	/	'Guido'
AUG	/	*L. pygmaea*
SEPT	sow 🖐	*L. tweedyi*
OCT	/	
NOV	transplant 🖐	
DEC	/	

CONDITIONS

Aspect These plants need full sun to thrive and if their position, the base of a wall perhaps, also reduces winter wet, all the better.

Site The soil must be fast draining, and to that end you must dig in plenty of horticultural sand or grit to provide the kind of conditions that the plant receives in its native California. Lewisias also enjoy reasonable fertility, with some added compost.

GROWING METHOD

Propagation Since lewesias freely hybridise, you do not have to do too much propagating. But you can propagate favourite colours by seed (except for the Cotyledon Hybrids) in the autumn, or pot up offsets in the summer.

Feeding Plants grown outside in the border might benefit from an early-spring application of a standard plant feed. Pot-grown lewisias, perhaps on a show bench in an alpine house, benefit from a mild liquid feed in the early spring.

Problems A fatal problem for lewisias is excessive moisture during the winter, otherwise watch out for slugs and snails. Remove them by hand each night to prevent the plants from becoming an instant salad.

FLOWERING

Season Lewisias are highly valued for their smallish tubular flowers, generally about 2.5cm (1in) across. They are most highly visible when the plant is growing in a crack in a wall. In the garden they would be rather lost.

LITHOPS
Living Stones

THIS CLUSTER of intricately patterned Lithops turbiniformis *is livened by a bright yellow flower.*

LOOKING JUST LIKE A MOUND OF PEBBLES, a large number of living stones fills this shallow bowl.

FEATURES

Sun

Living stones, stone plants, pebble plants and flowering stone are just a few of the common names assigned to these curious succulents. They are so completely camouflaged that it would be very easy to miss them entirely unless they were in flower. In their native south-west and South Africa, they generally grow buried in sand with only the tips of their leaves exposed. Their bodies are composed of a pair of very swollen, fleshy leaves on top of a fused double column with a gap or fissure along their length. The upper surfaces of the leaves are variously patterned and textured according to species and conditions. These plants are best grown in small pots where their curious shapes and markings can be observed. They make an excellent display.

LITHOPS AT A GLANCE

Astonishing tiny succulents in a wide range of colours and patterns. Highly collectible. 5°C (41°F) min.

		RECOMMENDED VARIETIES
JAN	/	*Lithops aucampiae*
FEB	/	*L. dorothea*
MAR	sow	*L. julii*
APR	transplant	*L. mormorata*
MAY	flowering	*L. karasmontana*
JUN	flowering	*L. salicola*
JULY	flowering	*L. schwantesii*
AUG	flowering	*L. turbiniformis*
SEPT	flowering	
OCT	/	
NOV	/	
DEC	/	

CONDITIONS

Aspect These plants should be grown in a position where there is full sun all day. They are best grown in pots on show benches in a glasshouse. They can cope with extreme heat, and attempts to shade them during the hottest part of the day are quite unnecessary.

Site The soil provided for living stones should drain very rapidly and small gravel or pebbles should be used as a mulch. Only use very fine pieces of gravel to set off the plants, though with some varieties it is tempting to camouflage them. It is amusing to let visitors see if they can distinguish between the real stones and the plants.

GROWING METHOD

Propagation These plants can be grown from divisions of offsets or from seed in spring to early summer. As living stones are not rapid growers, the clumps are best left undivided until they are about 10cm (4in) across.

Feeding Half-strength soluble liquid plant food can be given every 4–6 weeks through the active growth period.

Problems Most problems arise from overwatering or a poorly drained growing medium. Look out for ahpids when in flower.

FLOWERING

Season Flowers that emerge from the fissure of the living stone are daisy-like and yellow or white. They appear from late summer to mid-autumn in most species.

PACHYPODIUM LAMEREI
Madagascar Palm

A GREY-BROWN SPINY TRUNK topped with long, leathery leaves makes this a very curious-looking plant.

A FOCAL POINT in a succulent garden, Madagascar palm will grow to a stately height in suitable conditions.

FEATURES

Sun

Despite the common name of this most unusual plant, it is certainly not a palm and botanically shares none of the characteristics of palms. It has a trunk-like thick, spiny column, 3–6m (10–20ft) high, covered with honey-coloured tubercles bearing very sharp spines. The long dark green leaves up to 30cm (1ft) in length are rather heavily textured, but not succulent. These are arranged in a spiral formation on top of the column. The biggest surprise of all is the plant's frangipani-like fragrant white flowers, and in fact the Madagascar palm belongs to the same family as frangipani. This makes a wonderful feature plant for a succulent or desert glasshouse display. Most species of *Pachypodium* come from Madagascar, but a few are native to South Africa and south-west Africa. Easily grown, all you need is space.

PACHYPODIUM AT A GLANCE

P. lameri is startling dramatic tree-like succulent with creamy white summer flowers. 15°C (59°F) min.

		RECOMMENDED VARIETIES
JAN	/	*Pachypodium baronii*
FEB	/	*P. bispinosum*
MAR	sow ✍	*P. densiflorum*
APR	repotting ✍	*P. geayi*
MAY	transplant ✍	*P. lamerei*
JUN	flowering ❀	*P. namaquanum*
JULY	flowering ❀	*P. rosulatum*
AUG	/	*P. succulentum*
SEPT	/	
OCT	/	
NOV	/	
DEC	/	

CONDITIONS

Aspect Either grow this palm in a large pot or provide it with a special bed in a glasshouse or a conservatory. Its chief need is excellent light, so do not place it in a dark corner and resist growing exotic climbers against the windows as they will create too much shade. The palm also needs very good ventilation, with as much fresh air as possible on hot summer days.

Site The soil or potting mix must be perfectly drained. Potting mixes should contain about one-third organic matter.

GROWING METHOD

Propagation This plant is generally grown from seed sown in spring, but stem-tip cuttings can also be used.

Feeding Container-grown plants can benefit from a little slow-release fertiliser in the spring. Alternatively, scoop out the top third of soil in the pot and replace it with fresh compost. It is not sensible to overfeed a Madagascar palm, particularly if you have limited roof space, as it will outgrow its site.

Problems Madagascar palm suffers from only one severe problem. It is very prone to rotting if the drainage is not perfect or if the plant is ever overwatered.

FLOWERING

Season The lovely, smooth-petalled, white, fragrant flowers with their gold throats appear on top of the plant during the summer to early autumn period.

Seed pods Flowers are followed by twin seed pods that are shaped like bananas.

PEDILANTHUS TITHYMALOIDES
Zigzag Plant

A CURIOSITY FOR THE CONSERVATORY, the zigzag plant has crooked, dark green stems. Pink and white foliage variations become more evident in light or dappled shade. It has a string of common names including rick-rack plant, redbird flower, redbird cactus, ribbon cactus and devil's backbone.

FEATURES

Sun

Partial
Shade

This plant is in the *Euphorbiaceae* family, which means that it contains the poisonous milky latex that may cause skin irritations with some people. It is a clump-forming, upright, rather bushy shrub growing to about 2m (6ft) with thin, dark green zigzag stems. The plant's pointed leaves almost clasp the stems and may be evergreen or deciduous depending on conditions. The plain green-leaved form is less often cultivated than 'Variegatus', which has pink or white variegated foliage. This variegated form makes a fine feature in a succulent garden or it can be grown as an accent plant in a container.

PEDILANTHUS AT A GLANCE

P. tithymaloides is an excellent, striking conservatory plant specially in the variegated form with red bracts. 10°C (50°F) min.

		COMPANION PLANTS
JAN	/	
FEB	/	Aeonium
MAR	sow	*Crassula arborescens*
APR	/	Haworthia
MAY	transplant	*Kalanchoe pumila*
JUN	flowering	*Pachypodium lamerei*
JULY	flowering	*Sansevieria trifasciata*
AUG	flowering	*Sedum morganum*
SEPT	flowering	
OCT	/	
NOV	/	
DEC	/	

CONDITIONS

Aspect Zigzag plants grow best in full sun, but will tolerate partial shade.

Site These plants can be grown in any type of well-drained soil. In the wild they grow from southern parts of North America to the northern areas of South America, in Venezuela, and also in the West Indies. They grow in lowland, stony soil.

GROWING METHOD

Propagation This plant is easy to grow from stem tip cuttings taken during the warmer months. Cuttings must be dried off for a few days before planting. The plain green species can be grown from seed sown in spring.

Feeding A small amount of slow-release fertiliser can be applied in spring, or weak soluble liquid plant food can be given monthly through the growing season.

Problems This is generally a trouble-free group of plants. Provided you give the plant, which is related to euphorbias, moderately fertile soil and keep it on the dry side over winter it should flourish. Overwatering, especially when dormant, is the main cause of death.

FLOWERING

Season Flowers appear near stem tips in summer to autumn. The tiny greenish flowers are hooded with red bracts that have a yellow base.

PELARGONIUM OBLONGATUM
Pelargonium

A SURPRISE ADDITION to a collection of succulents is Pelargonium obligatum. *It is a marvellous plant with a good display of flowers in late spring and early summer. It is also an excellent plant for maintaining a continuous show of flowers in a collection of succulents.*

FEATURES

Sun

It might sound odd to include a pelargonium in a group of succulents, but about 220 of the 280-odd species are just that. (Do not confuse them with the hardy outdoor geraniums.) *Pelargonium oblongatum* comes from South Africa, in particular the northern region of Namaqualand. It was not actually collected until the early 19th century, making it quite a recent pelargonium since most of the others were collected well before this. It has a 15cm (6in) long oblong tuber (hence the Latin name), leaves with coarse hairs, and pale yellow flowers delicately feathered with maroon markings. It is definitely a collector's item, and could be the start of a collection with the orange-red *P. boranense* discovered in 1972 in Ethiopia, and *P. carnosum*, also from Namaqualand.

PELARGONIUM AT A GLANCE

P. oblongatum is a pelargonium with a difference. Try this species succulent with delicate pale yellow flowers. 2°C (36°F) min.

		RECOMMENDED VARIETIES
JAN	/	*Pelargonium abrotanifolium*
FEB	/	*P. cucullatum*
MAR	/	*P. fruticosum*
APR	repotting	*P. graveolens*
MAY	flowering	*P. papilionaceum*
JUN	flowering	*P. peltatum*
JULY	/	*P. radens*
AUG	/	*P. tomentosum*
SEPT	sow	
OCT	/	
NOV	transplant	
DEC	/	

CONDITIONS

Aspect The key requirement is bright sun; the more heat the better. In its native landscape it completely avoids any shade.

Site It needs to be grown in a pot where it can be properly cared for. Provide an open, free-draining compost. It is surprisingly easy to keep provided it is kept on the dry side while dormant in the summer. Active growth is as in the southern hemisphere, from autumn onwards. Leaf drop is in the spring.

GROWING METHOD

Propagation While it can be raised from seed, as with all pelargoniums stem cuttings give an extremely high success rate. Take them in mid-autumn, as new growth begins, and keep warm over winter avoiding a chilly windowsill. When mature, water well in the winter-spring period, with a reduction over summer.

Feeding Provide a mild fortnightly liquid feed when in full growth to boost the flowering show in the spring.

Problems Keep a check for aphids. They form tight packed clusters on the tasty young stems; spray accordingly. Once they take hold they can become quite a nuisance.

FLOWERING

Season There is a show of star-shaped flowers in the spring. After the bright blowsy colours with sharp reds and lipstick pinks of the more traditional pelargoniums like 'Happy Thought' they come as a quieter, interesting surprise.

SANSEVIERIA TRIFASCIATA
Mother-in-Law's Tongue

TUBULAR GREENISH FLOWERS *with a light perfume rise on tall, slender stems from the centre of mother-in-law's tongue.*

THE UPRIGHT LEAVES *are used here both as an edging and to screen the bare stems of the Hawaiian good luck plant behind them.*

FEATURES

Sun

Partial Shade

Also known as snake plant, the most commonly grown variety is 'Laurentii', which has cream to yellow bands down the sides of its tall, stemless, fleshy leaves. Mother-in-law's tongue used to be known as a rather neglected, indoor plant surviving in poor conditions, but it has now come out into the summer garden where it can provide foliage contrast and height in a succulent or mixed planting. It grows to over 1m (3ft) high and looks best once it has formed a good-sized clump. Leaves are dark green with paler irregular bands crosswise on the leaf, but there are many cultivars. 'Golden Hahnii' is a dwarf rosette form with broad yellow stripes on the leaf margins. Dwarf forms rarely exceed 15cm (6in) in height and are ideal for growing in pots.

SANSEVIERIA AT A GLANCE

S. trifasciata is an eye-catching plant with highly attractive leaves making dramatic summer bedding schemes. 13°C (55°F) min.

JAN	/	
FEB	/	
MAR	/	
APR	repotting	✍
MAY	flowering	✿
JUN	flowering	✿
JULY	flowering	✿
AUG	/	
SEPT	flowering	✿
OCT	/	
NOV	/	
DEC	/	

RECOMMENDED VARIETIES
Sansevieria trifasciata
      'Bantel's Sensation'
S. t. 'Golden Hahnii'
S. t. 'Hahnii'
S. t. 'Laurentii'
S. t. 'Silver Hahnii'

COMPANION PLANTS
Festuca glauca
Heliotrope
Iris
Ophiopogon

CONDITIONS

Aspect   This plant can be grown in full sun or partial shade, but the cream or yellow variegated forms may begin to revert to green if the light intensity is too low.

Site   Any type of soil is suitable for these plants, as long as it drains well. If planting out in a border for the summer, make sure that the soil conditions are not too radically different from those in the pot. Heavy, wet clay can easily be lightened if bags of horticultural sand or grit are dug in.

GROWING METHOD

Propagation   Plants multiply by spreading rhizomes or running roots that may be below or above the ground. They can be divided by separating these rhizomes, but these plants are also easily grown from leaf cuttings taken during the warmer months. The more you can propagate the better because mother-in-law's tongue makes an excellent bedding plant for the summer, possibly encircling a small island bed with a feature plant in the centre.

Feeding   Container-grown plants will benefit from the addition of slow-release fertiliser in spring.

Problems   Mother-in-law's tongue is usually almost indestructible. It is best not to over-water it.

FLOWERING

Season   Mature plants can produce greenish white scented flowers during the warmer months.

Berries   Berries may follow the flowers. These will ripen to orange.

SEDUM
Stonecrop

A POPULAR CONTAINER or rockery plant, the rarely seen stonecrop Sedum adolphii *takes on pink to red colours in cold weather.*

STARRY FLOWERS with intricate centres are a feature of stonecrop species. Colours include white, pink, red and yellow.

FEATURES

Sun

Partial Shade

Most plants in this large and diverse group of succulents are ideal for growing in pots, as well as in the garden where they can be used as edging, in rockeries or tucked into walls. *Sedum spectabile* is often planted in perennial borders where other succulents may look out of place. *S. sieboldii* has spreading stems and rarely exceeds 15cm (6in) in height. It has very attractive, almost round, blue-green leaves arranged in threes. It has a variegated green and gold form. *S. spathulifolium* forms a dense, low mat of small rosettes. Its variety 'Cape Blanco' has a white bloom on grey-green or purplish rosettes. *S. adolphii* has yellowish green, star-like rosettes with reddish hues at times. Although capable of growing to 30cm (1ft), it is more usually 20cm (8in) in height.

CONDITIONS

Aspect Full sun is best for most species, but some will tolerate light shade.

Site The soil or potting mix must be very well drained for these plants, and the addition of organic matter for garden plants will give them a decent boost, but only moderate levels are required.

GROWING METHOD

Propagation Division of plants is best done in the early spring. Cuttings can be taken at any time during the warm summer months.

Feeding Slow-release fertiliser or a little pelletted poultry manure given in the spring. In the main, they are best left alone with only a little cutting away of dead stems. Keep a watch at night for attacks by slugs and snails, especially when new spring growth is appearing.

Problems These plants are usually trouble-free.

FLOWERING

Season Flowering time depends on species, but many flower in summer-autumn. Flowers of several species are attractive to butterflies and bees, such as *S. spectabile* which has large flower heads of mauve-pink, rosy red or brick red on stems 40–60cm (16–24in) high in autumn. *S. sieboldii* has starry pink flowers that appear in masses in late summer or autumn. *S. adolphii* has starry flowers that are white. 'Ruby Glow' is a low-spreader with dark ruby red flowers appearing from mid-summer into the autumn, and 'Herbstfreude' produces marvellous pink autumn flowers that eventually turn copper-red.

SEDUM AT A GLANCE

About 400 species, from annuals to shrubs, with a terrific range of shapes and strong colours. Most hardy to -15°C (5°F).

JAN	/	**RECOMMENDED VARIETIES**
FEB	/	*Sedum cauticola*
MAR	/	'Herbstfreude'
APR	transplant	*S. kamtschaticum*
MAY	/	*S. morganianum*
JUN	/	'Ruby Glow'
JULY	flowering	*S. rubrotinctum*
AUG	flowering	*S. spectabile*
SEPT	flowering	*S. s.* 'Brilliant'
OCT	sow	*S. spurium* 'Schorbuser Blut'
NOV	/	'Vera Jameson'
DEC	/	

Sedum Morganianum
Burro's Tail

FEW GROWERS get to see flowers on their burro's tail plants. Very mature specimens bear dark flowers in spring.

THIS PLANT LOOKS MOST STRIKING when it is congested with masses of stems cascading from the pot or basket.

FEATURES

Partial Shade

The burro's tail is one succulent that must be grown in a hanging basket or in a pot set on a high shelf. In its Mexican habitat, it grows as a prostrate ground-covering plant.

It needs to be placed where it will not be accidentally knocked, as plants are quite brittle and leaves fall off easily—bare spots on the stem spoil the effect of the hanging stems. Leaves may also be shed if humidity is extremely low. Stems can trail down to a length of almost 1m (3ft) if conditions are ideal. Individual leaves are pale soft green and can be up to 2cm (¾in)long. They are slightly curved to clasp the stem, and look as if they have been plaited together. Sometimes the effect is yellow-green, sometimes silvery green.

SEDUM AT A GLANCE

S. morganianum is an excellent tumbling plant, with spring flowers, for a hanging basket. Easily grown. 7°C (45°F) min.

		RECOMMENDED VARIETIES
JAN	/	*Sedum cauticola*
FEB	/	'Herbstfreude'
MAR	transplant 🖐	*S. kamtschaticum*
APR	repotting 🖐	*S. k.* 'Variegatum'
MAY	flowering ❀	'Ruby Glow'
JUN	flowering ❀	*S. spectabile*
JULY	/	*S. s.* 'Brilliant'
AUG	/	'Vera Jameson'
SEPT	sow 🖐	
OCT	/	
NOV	/	
DEC	/	

CONDITIONS

Aspect   The plant absolutely demands a place in the shade to mimic its conditions in the wild. Light shade will do, but any more brightness is counter productive.

Site   The soil must be very fast draining or the plant will rot.

GROWING METHOD

Propagation   This plant is most easily grown from leaf cuttings, taken from spring to autumn, which should be dried for a day or two before planting. Even if you start off with one plant, it is best to propagate more so that the container will be filled.

Feeding   Apply granular slow-release fertiliser to containers in spring.

Problems   The two secrets of success are a shady position rather than a bright open one. And second, only water when the soil has dried out in the spring and summer. Watering over winter is very rarely necessary. This plant is quite capable of neglect, and can go a long period without a drink. Too much water, especially in the dormant winter months, leads to fatal rotting.

FLOWERING

Season   The small, starry flowers can be pale pink to dark red, and may be formed on the tips of mature stems. The flowers, when they appear, are usually borne in spring or summer, but burro's tail will only flower if the plant is very mature.

SEDUM RUBROTINCTUM
Sedum

ATTRACTIVE *all year round and easy to care for, the* Sedum rubrotinctum *is a plant with great appeal.*

IN COLD WEATHER *these excellent sedums may take on deep burgundy, scarlet, pink or purple tones.*

FEATURES

Partial Shade

Popular with both adults and children alike, this small succulent is virtually indestructible. It is easy to see why it is sometimes called the jellybean plant as the small pale green leaves are shaped like jellybeans and turn bright red in winter or when it is very dry. It can expand to a wide clump of 20cm (8in) or more in a season. Stems up to 25cm(10in) also branch upwards to carry the elongated rosettes of leaves. This is a good plant for a rockery, as a groundcover, or used in a border on the edge of a bed of cactuses and succulents. It is a very easy-care container plant and small pieces can be tucked into quaint ornamental pots with little soil. It also looks good in a wide shallow bowl.

SEDUM AT A GLANCE

S. rubrotinctum is a small spreading evergreen with gorgeous star-shaped yellow winter flowers. -5°C (23°F) min.

		RECOMMENDED VARIETIES
JAN	flowering ✿	*Sedum cauticola*
FEB	/	*S. kamtschaticum*
MAR	/	*S. morganianum*
APR	sow ✎	'Ruby Glow'
MAY	transplant ✎	*S. spectabile*
JUN	/	*S. s.* 'Brilliant'
JULY	/	*S. spurium* 'Schorbuser Blut'
AUG	/	'Vera Jameson'
SEPT	/	
OCT	/	
NOV	/	
DEC	flowering ✿	

CONDITIONS

Aspect *Sedum rubrotinctum* needs full sun for compact growth and good colour. However, it can also be grown in partial shade without detrimental effects. If grown indoors, make sure it is placed in a position where it receives sun for most of the day.

Site This plant can be grown in any type of well-drained soil or any general-purpose potting mix.

GROWING METHOD

Propagation Stems of this plant root downwards as they spread, and every leaf that drops or is broken off can form a new plant if it comes into contact with the soil. Individual leaves set upright in sand or seed-raising mix will readily make roots during warm weather.

Feeding Generally, fertilising is not needed for these plants, but a small amount of slow-release fertiliser can be applied in spring.

Problems *S. rubrotinctum* is generally trouble-free and is a good plant for beginner gardeners. It is virtually indestructible and the only way that it can be severely checked is by trying to grow it in wet clay. While it might survive the first summer, the first winter will result in instant rot. In cold areas, keep it frost free during the winter months.

FLOWERING

Season Star-shaped flowers are carried above the leaf rosettes. These should appear in the winter or during the spring.

SEMPERVIVUM
Houseleek

THIS HANDSOME, PURPLE-TIPPED hybrid houseleek needs no flowers to enhance its decorative effect.

GRADUALLY COLONISING an area of ground, this highly-attractive houseleek needs no special attention.

FEATURES

Sun

Houseleeks, especially the common houseleek *Sempervivum tectorum*, were once planted on roof tops both to hold slates in place and, it was believed, to provide protection against lightning. Most species are native to Europe, some have quite smooth leaves, and others are covered with soft hairs, while the cobweb houseleek, *S. arachnoideum*, is criss-crossed all over with white hairs. Houseleeks rarely grow more than 7.5–10cm (3-4in) high, but mats of rosettes can spread 60cm (2ft). These plants can be tucked into spaces in or on top of walls, or grown in containers or rockeries. Common houseleek and its numerous cultivars are the most frequently cultivated species. Several of the cultivars have burgundy foliage or leaves tipped with purple.

SEMPERVIVUM AT A GLANCE

Excellent decorative rock garden and wall plants, forming wide tactile carpets, demanding the sun. Hardy to -15°C (5°F).

		RECOMMENDED VARIETIES
JAN	/	*S. arachnoideum*
FEB	/	*S. a. tomentosum*
MAR	sow	*S. ciliosum*
APR	/	*S. giuseppii*
MAY	transplant	'Greenii'
JUN	flowering	'King George'
JULY	flowering	'Rubin'
AUG	flowering	'Othello'
SEPT	/	*S. tectorum*
OCT	/	
NOV	/	
DEC	/	

CONDITIONS

Aspect Plants grow best in the open in full sun with good air circulation.

Site Houseleeks must be grown in soil that is fast draining and open. If necessary, you could add coarse sand or grit to your soil. They particularly dislike having their roots kept wet over winter, which is why they thrive on the tops of walls.

GROWING METHOD

Propagation Plants are most easily grown by division of offsets taken in spring or summer. Houseleeks can be grown from seed, if available, which should be sown in spring. Although the rosettes may die after flowering, many offsets have usually been formed by this time and they can be replanted elsewhere or left where they are. They freely and prolifically hybridise creating new plants.

Feeding Low-nitrogen slow-release fertiliser may be applied as growth begins in spring. After that they require very little attention and no pampering.

Problems These plants are generally free of pest and disease problems if given the right climatic and growing conditions.

FLOWERING

Season Flowers of this plant may be yellow, red, purple or white depending on the species and are carried on upright stems above the rosette in summer. The rosettes may die off after flowering, but offsets will continue to grow.

SENECIO SERPENS
Senecio

THE FLESHY LEAVES of Senecio serpens *are pointed, but not prickly, making it good for groundcover.*

THE OUTSTANDING FOLIAGE of Senecio serpens *contrasts well with other plants. It stands out wherever it is planted.*

FEATURES

Sun

Partial Shade

This spreading succulent has fleshy upright foliage in the most unusual shade of blue. Possibly its most famous use is in the Blue Garden of Lotusland at Montecito in California, where it is grown with blue fescue and the blue-grey palm, *Brahea armata*. It tones well with other succulents that have a surface bloom on their leaves, and its nearly cylindrical leaves contrast well with shrubby or rosette-type plants. Branching from the base, the stems can grow to 30cm (1ft) high, but the plant is usually seen growing to 20cm (8in) or less with leaves about 3cm (1¼in) long. It's hard to believe this plant is in the daisy family, despite its small white flowers.

SENECIO AT A GLANCE

Shrubby perennial which likes poor conditions, famed for its bluish leaves. A collector's plant. 7°C (45°F) min.

JAN	/	
FEB	/	**RECOMMENDED VARIETIES**
MAR	sow	*Senecio articulatus* 'Variegatus'
APR	transplant	*S. cineraria* 'Silver Dust'
MAY	repotting	*S. c.* 'White Diamond'
JUN	/	*S. confusus*
JULY	flowering	*S. macroglossus* 'Variegatus'
AUG	flowering	*S. pulcher*
SEPT	/	*S. rowleyanus*
OCT	/	*S. viravira*
NOV	/	
DEC	/	

CONDITIONS

Aspect Its colour is best when this plant is grown in an open, sunny situation, but it can be also grown in light shade where the leaves will generally be taller.

Site The emphasis is on open, free-draining, poor soil. Avoid the rich and fertile which is completely counter-productive. You must replicate its unpampered conditions in the wild in South America, especially Chile and Argentina, and on the Falkland Islands.

GROWING METHOD

Propagation This plant is most easily grown from stem cuttings, taken from spring to mid-summer, which should be allowed to dry off for a few days before planting.

Feeding Senecio tolerates extremely poor soil but you may apply some slow-release fertiliser in spring if you want to give it a boost. Any more is totally unecessary. It benefits from being stood outside over the summer months.

Problems Generally trouble-free if the growing conditions are suitable.

FLOWERING

Season Small whitish-cream flowers appear in summer. These flowers add nothing to the plant, sometimes even detracting from its overall appearance, and are probably best removed unless you are waiting for the seed to set. Prune the stems off well behind the flower head.

YUCCA
Yucca

PURPLE-TINGED FOLIAGE is an attractive feature of this Yucca *species. This variety does not grow large and suits smaller gardens.*

THE RIGID GREY-GREEN leaves of Yucca whipplei *are sharply pointed. Its perfect symmetry of shape makes a great landscape feature.*

FEATURES

Sun

Yuccas are bold, architectural plants. Their stiff, upright leaves have sharp points, earning some the name of Spanish bayonet. They grow in rosette form with many reaching tree-like proportions and branching as they age—*Yucca aloifolia* to 8m (26ft) and the Joshua tree, *Y. brevifolia*, over 12m (40ft). *Y. filamentosa*, Adam's needle, has sword-like leaves about 75cm (30in) in length and edged with fine white curling threads. The species and its variegated forms are popular feature plants for smaller gardens. *Y. gloriosa*, growing to about 2m (6½ft) has blue-green leaves, while 'Variegata' has green foliage with wide yellow margins. *Y. whipplei*, or Our Lord's candle, has stiff, blue-green leaves and varies in its habit, but is most often seen around 1m (3ft) high.

YUCCA AT A GLANCE

Many big bold shapely plants that make excellent eye-catching features, some with amazing flowers. 7°C (45°F) min.

		RECOMMENDED VARIETIES
JAN	/	*Yucca aloifolia*
FEB	/	*Y. brevifolia*
MAR	sow 👈	*Y. elephantipes*
APR	/	*Y. filamentosa*
MAY	transplant 🌱	*Y. flaccida*
JUN	/	*Y. gloriosa*
JULY	flowering ✽	*Y. recurvifolia*
AUG	flowering ✽	*Y. whipplei*
SEPT	flowering ✽	
OCT	/	
NOV	/	
DEC	/	

CONDITIONS

Aspect These plants are best grown in an open, sunny position, where they should have plenty of room to show off their form. They do best when they are grown in a Mediterranean-type garden, or in a border where they have plenty of room to stand out, making an impact against nearby plants. If such a border is on a sunny, south-facing bank where the water quickly sluices away, then so much the better.

Site They can be grown in any type of soil as long as it is well drained. If unsure, dig in extra quantities of horticultural sand or grit.

GROWING METHOD

Propagation Seed of all the species can be sown in spring. Some plants can also be grown from suckers or division, or from root cuttings taken during warm weather.

Feeding Pelletted poultry manure or slow-release fertiliser can be applied in spring, but fertilising these plants is not usually essential. They are remarkably robust.

Problems Few, if any, problems. They only really fail to perform when grown in soil that is cold and wet during the winter.

FLOWERING

Season Most yuccas flower in summer or autumn, especially after soaking rain. The flowering spikes of yuccas are spectacular as they stand high above the foliage. The rounded or bell-shaped flowers are white, although sometimes they are flushed purple.

GROWING FOLIAGE PLANTS

Foliage plants have a lot to offer in both form and colour. These plants include the ornamental grasses which add a soft, natural look to the garden and supply movement as they sway and bend with the breeze. In complete contrast, some foliage plants are grown for their striking, architectural shapes and sword-like leaves. As features in the garden, foliage plants always stand out.

Foliage plants can be used to complement a variety of planting styles, perhaps enhancing or contrasting a textural theme. The great advantage of using foliage plants and grasses is that these plants do not always rely on the seasons to produce their best. Mostly, foliage plants and grasses are attractive all year round, adding shape to the winter garden.

KEY TO AT A GLANCE TABLES

PLANTING   FLOWERING

At a glance charts are your quick guide.
For full information, consult the accompanying text.

LEFT: Variegated liriope makes a pretty edging plant. These plants multiply and the clump will thicken up over a couple of seasons.

THE FOUNTAIN-LIKE GRASSY SEDGE, Carex buchananii, *from New Zealand makes an excellent shapely contrast to nearby perennials. The copper coloured foliage is also a good foil for green-leaved plants. This sedge is also grown on pond margins, making good reflections in the water.*

FOLIAGE PLANTS
IN GARDEN DESIGN

A garden of plants grown mainly for their shape, texture and foliage colour can be just as interesting as a garden filled with flowers. Many foliage plants are grown as accents or features. They have sculptural or architectural qualities that add a special dimension to the garden—big, striking plants such as the *Paulownia tomentosa* are good examples.

An all-green garden can be an inviting, restful haven; consider the range of tones of green that are available as well as the foliage types that can be found. Contrast ferns with large-leaved *Fatsia japonica*, or plant the splayed leaves of the Chusan palm through the vertical growth of *Phormium tenax*. In fact, tall-growing species of *Phormium tenax* make excellent screens or windbreaks and are perfect as a backdrop for smaller shrubs or perennials. The many coloured forms of flax now available can make a garden feature by themselves. These and many other foliage plants also make excellent container plants.

ORNAMENTAL GRASSES

The grass family contains a huge number and range of plants, from those used as lawn grasses through to small tufty ornamentals such as blue fescue and, at the other extreme, the towering giant bamboos. The impetus for including ornamental grasses in home gardens and larger landscapes came from Germany and the United States, and even though the last 20 years has seen an enormous increase in the use of grasses in the garden, many people still feel uncertain about them. General nurseries do not often carry more than eight types, but more and more specialist nurseries are stocking an increasing range of interesting possibilities. Grasses have a lot to offer, both in form and colour, adding a soft natural look. They can be used as features, fillers, groundcovers, edging plants and screens. And by not cutting them back at the end of autumn, they contribute additional forms to the winter garden, especially when covered in frost.

Designers tend to use grasses in one of two ways. Either they make punctuation marks in the border, or a kind of division, where once box topiary might have been used. Big clumpy plants like *Stipa gigantea* are an obvious choice. And such repeat planting down a border helps draw the eye on to the end. Or they are being increasingly used in continuous, loose flowing sequences, much as they grow in the wild, emphasising a natural, unfussy look. A block of *Molinia caerulea arundinacea* looks sensational when it turns amber in the autumn.

Grasses add upright, simple shapes to the landscape, and as they bend with every breeze they also add movement. The many colours of grasses go beyond the numerous shades of green to include blue or blue-green, red, russet, purple, yellow and silver, and the big range of variegated forms with cream or yellow stripes and margins. The plumes of the flowering spikes of grasses stand high above the clumps, adding another decorative feature.

Many of the ornamental grasses are herbaceous, dying back in winter, ensuring that each season's new growth is fresh and lovely. Most are very easy to maintain as they require only to be slashed back to the ground in winter or early spring to allow the new growth to be seen at its best.

GROWING NEEDS

Apart from sedges, the vast majority of grasses and plants used for their foliage prefer to be grown in a moderately rich soil that is also well drained. Plants grown in containers will need a good-quality potting mix that is also fast draining. Many of these foliage plants and grasses are long lived, so attention to soil preparation before planting will pay dividends in the future. Whatever type of soil you have, it will be greatly improved by digging in large quantities of decayed manure or compost a couple of weeks before planting. If you are planting in winter, do this at least a month ahead.

It is impossible to give general directions about such a diverse range of plants but with most members of this group, you should water the plants immediately after planting and continue to water regularly until you can see that they are putting on new growth. Many plants tolerate long, dry periods well, while others will always need water through dry summer months. Some may benefit from the use of fertiliser through their first growing season, and potted plants will in the main need feeding throughout their lives. Other plants dislike any supplementary feeding at all.

Maintenance

Most ornamental grasses and foliage plants will need little continuous maintenance, but it is important to keep plants looking their best as you are relying on their form and foliage for effect. Spend a little time grooming your plants to make them look as good as possible. Pulling off or pruning out dead foliage makes a big difference, as does the removal of flowering stems that are past their peak. In hot summers, the flowering spikes of grasses can start to look very tatty by the autumn, but more usually they keep their form longer and can be left for 'frosting', which gives a marvellous effect. Some grasses can be cut back easily with secateurs, but if you have tough plants or a lot of them you may need to use a strimmer.

PROPAGATION

A great many of the plants covered in the this book are propagated by division of existing clumps. Coloured or variegated forms of the species must be grown by separation of divisions, as the seed may be sterile and most likely will not grow true to type. Some plants can only be grown from seed, while others will not set seed at all unless they happen to be cultivated in their native habitat. If you want a labour-saving garden with just the occasional tidy up, pulling dead leaves out of clumps of leaves, and a spring cut back in order to let new growth shoot up and emerge, then a grass-based garden is just what you need. Colourful, shapely, stylish, vigorous and whispy, it can be amazingly beautiful and varied.

WHAT CAN GO WRONG?

Grasses are remarkably free of pest and disease problems. Some of the foliage plants described in the following pages may have a few specific problems, but generally, these are a trouble-free group of plants. Any specific problems will be covered in individual entries.

THE DECORATIVE COLUMNS of small, shiny seed capsules on mat rush are punctuated with small spines.

THE SHAPELY SILVER FOLIAGE of cardoon makes a good foil for more sombre greens in the garden.

ARTEMISIA
Wormwood

THE LACY GREY FOLIAGE of Artemisia 'Powis Castle' is its great attraction. Yellow flowers in summer add little to its appeal.

GROWN AS A LOW HEDGE, the cultivar 'Powis Castle' can be used effectively with plants of any colour or foliage type.

FEATURES

Sun

Grey- and silver-leaved plants light up a garden and provide a foil for brightly coloured flowers. They also make wonderful accent plants in mixed borders. Varieties of ornamental wormwoods have silvery grey, silky foliage that may be soft and lacy, feathery, fern-like or in narrow ribbons. Some wormwoods grow rather upright, but most give the effect of rounded frothy clumps of foliage about 1m (3ft) high and wide. Wormwood has been used since ancient Egyptian times as, among other things, a moth and insect repellent, and was formerly much used in folk medicine. *Artemesia absinthium*, although still used to flavour various liqueurs and aperitifs and wines, is quite poisonous if taken in all but minute quantities.

ARTEMISIA AT A GLANCE

Grown for their fashionable greyish-silvery and often feathery foliage. Excellent border plants. Most hardy to -15°C (5°F).

		RECOMMENDED VARIETIES
JAN	/	*Artemisia abrotanum*
FEB	/	*A. absinthium*
MAR	/	'Lambrook Silver'
APR	sow 👆	*A. alba* 'Canascens'
MAY	/	*A . dracunculus*
JUN	transplant 👆	*A. lactiflora*
JULY	flowering ✿	*A. pontica*
AUG	flowering ✿	'Powis Castle'
SEPT	sow 👆	*A. stelleriana* 'Boughton Silver'
OCT	/	
NOV	/	
DEC	/	

Varieties   Southernwood, A. abrotanum, with very fine grey-green foliage, is grown ornamentally but also in herb gardens. The species A. absinthium and A. arborescens have finely cut, aromatic foliage, but more popular are the cultivars 'Lambrook Silver', which has very deeply divided silver foliage and a fairly upright habit, and 'Powis Castle', which is dense and billowing with fine, lacy, grey-silver leaves.

CONDITIONS

Aspect   These plants must have full sun all day and exposure to good air circulation.

Site   Plants will grow in poor soil, but it must be well drained. If grown in solid heavy clay the plants will quickly die. Such soil can be broken up with horticultural sand and grit.

GROWING METHOD

Propagation   Plants may be short lived, but are easily grown from firm tip cuttings taken any time through the warmer months. Once potted up they quickly develop good root systems. It is worth taking cuttings of the slightly more tender plants like 'Powis Castle' in case they are killed off in a severe winter.

Feeding   Best grown without supplementary fertiliser as these plants are adapted to poor soils.

Problems   Wormwoods are generally trouble-free.

FLOWERING

Season   Most plants produce small daisy-type flowers above the foliage in summer.

CANNA
Indian shot plant

THE BEST WAY TO ADD starting height, shape and colour to the summer garden is by planting out a group of tropical Cannas. The best have flamboyant, paddle-shaped leaves and gorgeous coloured flowers that are just like a Sladidi's. The more you can plant the better.

FEATURES

Sun

Cannas give an excellent exotic twist to the garden. They are half-hardy, rhizomatous perennials which need cutting down in the autumn before the frosts, and storing over winter. They have large, colourful leaves up to 2m (6ft) high and relatively small flowers which range from quiet pink to shrieking red and orange. *Canna* 'Striata' has eye-catching orange flowers and green and yellow striped leaves. 'Black Knight' has rich purple foliage with crimson flowers, and others like 'Endeavour' have fresh green foliage. Breeders are currently trying to produce a white flowering canna. The plants are best used as the focal point in a bedding scheme in gardens featuring other large-leaved or colourful plants like bananas, coleus and dahlias.

CANNA AT A GLANCE

Dramatic, eye-catching bedding plants with big leaves topped by small, often startling bright flowers. Hardy to 0°C (32°F).

		RECOMMENDED VARIETIES
JAN	/	*Canna* 'Black Knight'
FEB	/	'Durban'
MAR	sow	'En Avant'
APR	dividing	*C. iridiflora*
MAY	transplant	'Lucifer'
JUN	/	'Praetoria'
JULY	flowering	'Striata'
AUG	flowering	'Wyoming'
SEPT	flowering	
OCT	/	
NOV	/	
DEC	/	

CONDITIONS

Aspect Cannas prefer a sunny position, well away from the shade. It is important to avoid a windy site, however, or the leaves will get badly flayed.

Site The plants are quite hungry and the soil needs to be fairly rich. During hot dry spells you will need to water well to counter any moisture loss from the large leaves.

GROWING METHOD

Propagation The best way to increase stock is by dividing the rhizomes in the spring, making sure each section has the 'eye' of a new shoot. These can be planted up, with gentle watering at first, and gradually hardened off before they are planted out.

Feeding Add well-rotted compost before planting, or an all-purpose fertiliser in the spring and again in the summer.

Problems The two potential summer pests are caterpillars and slugs. Keep an eye out for both. When grown under glass cannas can suffer badly from red spider mite. The tell-tale sign is a speckling on the leaves, and in bad cases mini spiders' webs.

FLOWERING

Season The gladiolus-like flowers appear from mid-summer until the early autumn. Cultivars like 'En Avant' have yellow flowers spotted with orange. The quieter tones of species varieties are also very beautiful. *Canna iridiflora,* for example, is a subtle lipstick pink.

CAREX
Sedges

TINY DARK FLOWERS are starting to appear on this variegated form of the fine-leaved sedge, Carex brunii.

*THE FOUNTAIN-LIKE GROWTH of a sedge is ideal as a filler in front of Californian lilac (*Ceanothus *species).*

FEATURES

Sun

Partial
Shade

With a range of habitats from the coast to the mountains, there is probably a sedge to suit every possible garden situation. Although traditionally associated with wet areas, they also tolerate dry conditions. There is a great range of foliage colour, from every shade of green to reds and browns, yellow, silver and variegated. Their growth habit varies, too, from compact miniatures through to tussock growers to the tall, flowing types. For a splash of brilliant yellow colour, Bowles' golden sedge, *Carex elata* 'Aurea', is probably the best. Growing to 60cm (2ft) in height, the rich, golden leaves have narrow, green margins. *C. comans* is a much smaller perennial, just 25cm (10in) by 75cm (30in), which has very fine, hair-like leaves.

CAREX AT A GLANCE

Highly valued perennials which are essential for any garden which is well stocked with quality grasses. Hardy to -5°C (23°F).

		RECOMMENDED VARIETIES
JAN	/	*Carex comans*
FEB	/	*C. elata* 'Aurea'
MAR	sow	*C. morrowii* 'Fisher's Form'
APR	/	*C. oshimensis* 'Evergold'
MAY	divide	*C. petriei*
JUN	transplant	*C. pendula*
JULY	flowering	*C. riparia* 'Variegata'
AUG	flowering	'Silver Sceptre'
SEPT	divide	*C trifida*
OCT	/	
NOV	/	
DEC	/	

Varieties — Drooping sedge, *C. pendula*, forms a wide clump growing to 1.2m (4ft). Its blue-green foliage arches downwards and the dark brown flower catkins droop attractively beyond the clump. *C. testacea* has foliage that emerges green, changes to orange, and turns a pinky copper colour at maturity. The narrow cascading foliage grows to about 40cm (16in), making it ideal for edges of rockeries.

CONDITIONS

Aspect — Most species do well in full sun or light shade.
Site — Moisture-retentive soils containing plenty of organic matter are ideal, but sedges will adapt to almost any soil type. However, with quick-draining soil it is worth digging in plenty of well-rotted manure to improve conditions.

GROWING METHOD

Propagation — Clumps can be lifted and divided in the spring. Species can be grown from seed sown in spring. It is worth building up your collection and planting sedges in groups all over the garden, creating an informal unity.
Feeding — Fertiliser is not usually needed. Add manure or a compost mulch only if the soil is very poor.
Problems — These plants are generally trouble-free.

FLOWERING

Season — Flowering spikes of some species are most decorative. Both the foliage and the flowers make a useful addition to a cut flower display.

CLEMATIS ARMANDII
Clematis

A CREAMY WHITE mass of flowers in mid-spring on Clematis armandii shows up well against its evergreen foliage.

FEATURES

Sun

Partial
Shade

A highly distinctive and eye-catching evergreen clematis introduced in 1900 by the plant hunter Ernest Wilson from China. It has dark green, glossy leaves 13cm (5in) long and 5cm (2in) wide and can grow about 5m (15ft) high. It clambers up and over frames or shrubs using tendrils which tightly wrap around any available structure or stem. Do not attempt to constrain it. In late winter in sheltered areas clusters of flower buds begin to swell, and on opening in the spring they release a sweet scent. 'Apple Blossom' has leaves with a marked bronze tint. There is another form called 'Snowdrift' which is said to be a slight improvement on the species. The flowers are shaped like five-pointed stars.

CLEMATIS AT A GLANCE

C. armandii is famed for its shapely evergreen leaves, and scented spring flowers. Hardy to -5°C (23°C).

JAN	/	RECOMMENDED VARIETIES
FEB	/	*Clematis alpina*
MAR	/	*C. cirrhosa* var. *balearica*
APR	flowering ❀	'Doctor Ruppel'
MAY	mulch	'Etoile Violette'
JUN	tie in	*C. flammula*
JULY	tie in	'Jackmanii'
AUG	/	*C. montana*
SEPT	/	*C. tangutica*
OCT	/	
NOV	/	
DEC	/	

CONDITIONS

Aspect The key to success is a warm, sheltered position. Do not grow it where it is exposed to raw, cold winds because they will flay and ruin the leaves, its chief attraction.

Site Like all clematis it likes its roots in the shade and its head in the sun.

GROWING METHOD

Propagation This is notoriously hard which explains why the plant costs about twice as much as any other clematis. Though cuttings root easily they do not always shoot. The result is a pot full of roots with very little above. Grafting onto a stock plant is very successful but is best left to professional nurserymen.

Feeding Provide a rich soil that has had plenty of well-rotted compost dug into it before planting. Keep the compost away from the climber's roots. In following years a general purpose spring feed is fine. Water well in hot dry summers.

Problems Once this clematis takes off there is no stopping it. Try to make sure that you train it up towards the light, spreading it well out, stopping new growth from disappearing into nearby hedges.

FLOWERING

Season Mature plants in early spring are liberally covered in a mass of white flowers releasing a pervasive, soft perfume. Sheltered spots which are not struck by fierce spring frosts give the best results.

CORDYLINE AUSTRALIS
Cabbage Palm

A MULTI-BRANCHED cabbage tree is massed with cream to beige flower spikes. It will make a dramatic presence.

ALTHOUGH NATIVE TO NEW ZEALAND, this cabbage tree complements the Mediterranean flavour of white walls and terracotta.

FEATURES

Sun

Partial Shade

This New Zealand native is sometimes called palm lily or cabbage palm because of its resemblance to palms, even though it is no relation. Growing very upright when young, it branches as it ages and matures, but these branches are thick and not numerous. The palm is capable of growing to 10m (33ft) or so in ideal conditions but is most often seen in gardens at around 3m (10ft). This is a good feature plant for both its size and form, lending itself to garden or container cultivation at least when young. The rather tough, sword-shaped leaves emerge stiff and upright but become pendulous as they age. The leaves are plain mid-green in the species, and there are a number of cultivars.

CORDYLINE AT A GLANCE

C. australis is a big, showpiece, architectural palm-like tree with stiff leaves topping a tall bare trunk. Hardy to -5°C (23°F)

		RECOMMENDED VARIETIES
JAN	/	*Cordyline australis* 'Albertii'
FEB	/	*C. a.* 'Atropurpurea'
MAR	/	*C. a.* 'Coffee Cream'
APR	/	*C. a.* 'Purple Tower'
MAY	sow	*C. a.* 'Red Star'
JUN	transplant	*C. a.* 'Sundance'
JULY	flowering	*C. a.* 'Torbay Dazzler'
AUG	flowering	*C. banksii*
SEPT	/	*C. indivisa*
OCT	/	
NOV	/	
DEC	/	

Varieties   'Variegata' has creamy white striped leaves, 'Purple Tower' has broad, purple foliage, and 'Albertii' has red leaf margins and midribs with cream stripes on the leaves. The Australian, *Cordyline stricta*, grows to 2m (6ft) with long dark leaves and white to purple flowers, followed by purple-black berries.

CONDITIONS

Aspect   Grow in full sun or partial shade. Foliage colour may be more intense in filtered light.

Site   Soil must be well drained and should be enriched with organic matter before planting.

GROWING METHOD

Propagation   Can be grown from seed, suckers or stem cuttings taken in spring or summer. While mature plants can withstand dry spells, young plants should always be well watered during long hot summers.

Feeding   Apply pelletted poultry manure or complete plant food in spring. Potted plants should have slow-release fertiliser or monthly applications of liquid plant food in the growing season.

Problems   Generally easy to grow and free of problems. The only possible problem is under glass where red spider mite can strike.

FLOWERING

Season   Mature plants bear long sprays of creamy white flowers in summer.

Berries   Small white or mauve-tinted berries are produced after flowering.

CYNARA CARDUNCULUS

Cardoon

VERY SIMILAR TO the Scottish thistle, the strongly serrated margins and well-defined veins are equally a feature of the silver-grey cardoon.

STIFF FLOWER BUDS yet to open and colour are forming on the stem tips of this mature clump of cardoon.

FEATURES

Sun

This striking-looking plant is the perfect accent plant to provide a sculptural shape of silver-grey foliage. Growing to about 1.5m (5ft) high and wide, cardoon is a herbaceous perennial that dies back to the ground in winter. This is not a plant for a very small garden as it might tend to be overpowering in such a confined situation. It is best viewed against a range of other foliage colours and shapes. The slightly spiny leaves can be up to 50cm (20in) long, the margins deeply lobed or incised. When the plant produces its purple, thistle-like flowers, the resemblance to its near relative, the globe artichoke, can be seen. Cardoon is edible, too. The fleshy leaf bases can be tied in bundles, blanched and eaten either as they are or cooked, like celery.

CYNARA AT A GLANCE

C. cardunculus is a big perennial with purple, thistle-like summer flowers and large, spiny leaves. Hardy to -15°C (5°F)

		COMPANION PLANTS
JAN	/	
FEB	/	Acanthus
MAR	/	*Crambe cordifolia*
APR	divide 👈	*Eryngium bourgatii*
MAY	/	Euphorbia
JUN	flowering ✿	*Fatsia japonica*
JULY	flowering ✿	*Gunnera manicata*
AUG	flowering ✿	*Melianthus major*
SEPT	flowering ✿	Rodgersia
OCT	/	
NOV	/	
DEC	/	

CONDITIONS

Aspect Cardoon grows best in full sun all day, but avoid any windy open situations where the foliage gets flayed and shredded.

Site The soil must be well drained and should be heavily enriched with manure or compost before planting.

GROWING METHOD

Propagation Divide the clumps or separate suckers in early spring. Cardoon can also be grown from spring-sown seed, but the plants may vary greatly. The former method is by far the best bet for the impatient.

Feeding Apply complete plant food or scatterings of pelleted poultry manure in spring and mid-summer. The cardoon is a hungry feeder, also needing plenty of water during hot dry spells to perform to its best.

Problems No specific pest or disease problems are known to trouble this plant.

FLOWERING

Season The purple, thistle-like flowers of cardoon are carried on stems 1.5m (5ft) high and resemble its relative, the globe artichoke. The flowers appear in summer and can be allowed to dry on the plant if they are destined for indoor decoration, or they can be removed from the plant when they are past their prime and begin to look unsightly. In fact, many remove the flower stems the moment they appear so that all the plant's energy goes into producing its architectural foliage.

ENSETE VENTRICOSUM

Abyssinian Banana

BRIGHT CRIMSON MIDRIBS are a distinguishing feature of the large bold leaves of Abyssinian banana.

A TROPICAL ATMOSPHERE is instantly created by the marvellous presence of these imposing, bold-leaved plants.

FEATURES

Sun

Partial
Shade

With its huge paddle-shaped leaves, this fast-growing plant brings a tropical touch to the garden. Its foliage effect is spectacular. It may be grown in containers in glasshouses and brought outdoors and plunged into a garden bed to be the highlight of a summer display. This plant can grow to 5.5m (18ft) high and several metres wide. Its bold, rich green leaves are highlighted by midribs that are bright crimson beneath; the leaves form a distinct crown above the thick, trunk-like bases. The form 'Maurelii' is even more attractive because it has a marked red tinge on top of the leaves as well as underneath them. Although the true flowers are not showy, they are enclosed within bronze to reddish bracts. Following flowering, which may occur after three to four years of growth, individual plants die and are then cut off at ground level.

ENSETE AT A GLANCE

E. ventricosum is a splendid tropical perennial with paddle-shaped summer leaves growing 4.3m (14ft) long. 7°C (45°F) min.

		COMPANION PLANTS
JAN	/	
FEB	/	Agave
MAR	sow	Bamboo
APR	/	Canna
MAY	transplant	Datura
JUN	/	*Fatsia japonica*
JULY	flowering	*Melianthus major*
AUG	flowering	*Musa basjoo*
SEPT	/	*Paulownia tomentosa*
OCT	/	Yucca
NOV	/	
DEC	/	

CONDITIONS

Aspect Abyssinian banana is equally at home in full sun or in partial shade. To look its best, this plant needs to be sheltered from very strong wind, which tends to rip and spoil the foliage. In open, exposed windy gardens you will need to provide an effective shelter belt.

Site The ideal soil for this plant is one that is very well drained, but also has been enriched with organic matter.

GROWING METHOD

Propagation Masses of seed are produced in warm climates. Sow seed in spring after soaking overnight in warm water. That said, it is far easier to buy a new plant than to raise one.

Feeding Give these plants some pelleted poultry manure and organic mulches in spring and again in summer. When it is pot grown, the Abyssinian banana needs to be given a monthly liquid feed. This should ensure that it always looks its best.

Problems No specific pest or disease problems are known to trouble this plant. In hot summers, it is a gross drinker, compensating for evaporation from its huge leaves.

FLOWERING

Season In the wild, white flowers, which usually appear in summer, are mostly concealed within the showy reddish bronze bracts. Individual plants die after flowering.

Fruits Flowers are followed by a dry, banana-like fruit containing the seeds. The seeds of Abyssinian banana – along with the flower heads – are cooked and eaten in Africa.

ERYNGIUM
Sea holly

THE EYECATCHING SEA HOLLIES *really jazz up a border, adding thistle-like shapes but beware of planting them right at the edge if children are about. The spines can be extremely sharp. The best hollies have excellent blue colouring.*

FEATURES

Sun

Sea holly is a 230-species strong genus, with annuals, biennials and perennials. Though they are related to cow parsley they bear no resemblance, being grown for their marvellous, attractive, spikey appearance, blue flowers (especially the new 'Jos Eijking'), and an ability to thrive in poor, rocky, sunny ground. Heights can vary considerably from *E. alpinum* at 70cm (28in) tall, which as its name suggests grows in the Alps, to *E. eburneum* from South America which can reach 1.5m (5ft), and *E. pandanifolium* which is much taller at 3m (10ft). One of the most attractive is *E. variifolium* which has rounded, white-veined foliage and pale blue flowers. It grows 35cm (14in) high.

ERYNGIUM AT A GLANCE

Fashionable perennials both for their striking shapes and use in Mediterranean-type gardens. Hardy to -18°C (64°F)

JAN	/	RECOMMENDED VARIETIES
FEB	sow	*Eryngium alpinum*
MAR	divide	*E. a.* 'Blue Star'
APR	transplant	*E. bourgatii*
MAY	transplant	*E. b.* 'Oxford Blue'
JUN	flowering	*E. giganteum*
JULY	flowering	'Jos Eijking'
AUG	flowering	*E.* x *oliverianum*
SEPT	sow	*E.* x *tripartium*
OCT	/	
NOV	/	
DEC	/	

CONDITIONS

Aspect Grow in full sun, well out of the shade.

Site There are basically two types of sea holly, with different growing needs. The majority, such as *E. alpinum* and the excellent *E. bourgati* and its cultivars, prefer fast-draining, fertile ground, while some, including *E. eburneum*, need much poorer stonier ground, so that their roots are well clear of the cold winter wet. Also note that many sea hollies have vicious spines on the leaves. Keep them well clear of areas where children play

GROWING METHOD

Propagation Sow the seed when ripe. Alternatively, get quicker results by taking root cuttings in late winter. You can also divide established clumps in the spring.

Feeding Only the first kind of sea holly, needing fertile ground, benefits from a spring feed, and some well-rotted manure. Good drainage is still important though.

Problems Slugs and snails are the main problems when sea holly is grown in the border, damaging the new young leaves. Promptly remove when seen, or use a chemical treatment.

FLOWERING

Season Some sea hollies flower in early summer, while others last from mid-summer to early or even mid-autumn in very dry weather. Cut back the spent stems after flowering.

Cutting Sea holly make invaluable cut flowers. They also make exceptional dried arrangements, combined with other, softer flowers.

EUPHORBIA
Spurge

EVERY GARDEN SHOULD HAVE A SPURGE. They can make excellent feature plants, with strong architectural shapes, standing out against contrasting plants, or taking up the kind of space normally reserved for a big colourful pot.

FEATURES

Sun

Partial Shade

Perennial euphorbias, both evergreen and deciduous, will grow in a wide range of conditions. They tend to be quite sturdy and many of them lean at 45 degrees. The foliage is often of a very high quality, with horizontal 'fingers' pointing out, later surpassed by the coloured cyathia in the summer. They are often lime or yellow green, and in the case of *E. characias* have a purple-black centre, and with *E. x martinii* they are dark red. The orange-red involucres can be even more eye grabbing. Spurges are becoming increasingly fashionable, giving strong structure and shape. Some though, like *E. ferox,* with nasty thorns, need to be treated with obvious care. And when cut all euphorbias exude a milky sap which is a strong irritant.

EUPHORBIA AT A GLANCE

A genus of some 2,000 species with many excellent plants for a cottage or modern, stylish architectural garden. Hardy to -18°C (0°F).

		RECOMMENDED VARIETIES
JAN	/	*Euphorbia* amygdaloides
FEB	/	*var.* robbiae
MAR	divide	*E. characias*
APR	transplant	*E. c.* 'Lambrook Gold'
MAY	flowering	*E. griffithii* 'Dixter'
JUN	flowering	*E. x martinii*
JULY	flowering	*E. myrsinites*
AUG	flowering	*E. palustris*
SEPT	flowering	*E. polychroma*
OCT	sow	*E. schillingii*
NOV	/	
DEC	/	

CONDITIONS

Aspect
Check your plant's requirements before planting it out. With so many different varieties to consider, these may vary considerably. Some spurges like a site in full sun, while others prefer a slightly shaded position.

Site
Again, depending on the chosen plant, provide either light, fast-draining soil or ground which is much more damp and moist, and which has had plenty of leaf-mould dug into it.

GROWING METHOD

Propagation
The slow method is sowing seed when ripe, or the following spring. Far quicker, divide the perennials in the spring, making sure each section has a good root system. Alternatively, take cuttings from late spring to mid-summer.

Feeding
Those spurges which require rich soil can be given a scattering of complete plant food in the spring, when they also need to be mulched. Those spurges which require fast-draining ground need only be fed.

Problems
Aphids and slugs are two possible problems. Birds should eat the aphids - if not, spray. Slugs or snails should be picked off at night and destroyed.

FLOWERING

Season
Flowers appear in spring or summer.

Cutting
They make good cut flowers, but avoid contact with irritant sap by wearing gloves and goggles. Cut back brown stems in autumn to encourage new growth.

FARFUGIUM JAPONICUM
Leopard Plant

THE GOLD-SPLASHED LEAVES of Farfugium japonicum light up the garden even when grown under trees.

FARFUGIUM GROWS behind a standard azalea. It is teamed here with winter rose and groundcovering campanula.

FEATURES

Partial Shade

Although there are several variegated cultivars of this plant, the most widely planted and the one sometimes known as leopard plant is *Farfugium japonicum* 'Aureomaculatum'. This is an excellent plant to use as a tall groundcover or as a feature to light up shady corners of the garden. A single specimen has little effect; it is most striking when several plants are grouped together. It also lends itself well to container growing. Growing 40–60cm (16–24in) high, the large kidney-shaped leaves are a rich, glossy green, heavily spotted or splashed gold. In good conditions, leaves can be up to 25cm (10in) across, but they are more often about 15cm (6in). Growing from an underground rhizome, the leaves are held high on soft, thick stems that are covered in powdery bloom.

FARFUGIUM AT A GLANCE

F. japonicum is a rarely grown, terrific Japanese foliage plant with strongly variegated forms. Hardy to -5°C (23°F).

		COMPANION PLANTS
JAN	/	Crocosmia
FEB	/	Geranium
MAR	sow	Grasses
APR	divide	Hedera
MAY	transplant	Iris
JUN	/	Narcissus
JULY	/	Penstemon
AUG	/	Pulmonaria
SEPT	divide	
OCT	/	
NOV	/	
DEC	/	

CONDITIONS

Aspect
Grows best in dappled sunlight or light shade. It requires some shelter from strong wind.

Site
The soil should be well drained and heavily enriched with manure or compost. Mulch plants well with organic matter.

GROWING METHOD

Propagation
The best way to increase your stock of plants is to divide them. Only plant them out in wild areas, otherwise grow them in pots. You can also propagate by seed, sowing in a cold frame in the autumn or in mid spring.

Feeding
Apply pelleted poultry manure or complete plant food in spring. Provided the soil was well enriched with rotted manure before planting though, it is unlikely that the ground will need too many extra nutrients.

Problems
Snails find the foliage of this plant very attractive, so take precautions. No other problems are commonly found.

FLOWERING

Season
The yellow, daisy-like flowers that appear above the large leaves seem 'out of place' and do not enhance the decorative effect of this foliage plant. This is certainly true of the excellent 'Argenteum' and 'Aureomaculatum' with their large, kidney-shaped variegated leaves. You can cut off the flowers as they appear, but it is a personal choice. The flowers appear from summer onwards, depending on climate.

FARGESIA PHYLLOSTACHYS
Bamboo

THE FARGESIAS INCLUDE *some of the hardiest bamboos for the garden. They are generally non-invasive.*

THE PHYLLOSTACHYS OFFER *some of the most attractive bamboos, several with striking orange and even striped stems.*

FEATURES

Sun

Partial Shade

Many people who have suffered the horrors of invading bamboo are appalled at the idea of anyone growing it from choice. However, there are many ornamental bamboos that are not invasive and even some of the running types can be easily confined. Bamboos make lovely features for large gardens and parks, and also can be used very effectively as attractive windbreaks and screens. They range in size from the dwarf forms that may only grow to 60cm (2ft) in height up to the massive, bamboos that grow to 30m(100ft) high in the wild with canes 15cm (6in) across. Bamboos may be clumping (sympodial) or running (monopodial). It is not advisable to plant running bamboos in a small space as their underground runners (rhizomes) can travel 1.8m (6ft) in a single growing season.

Garden uses There are three basic kinds of bamboo. Tall, thickish canes, 3.7m (12ft) high and over. They are smart with dramatic colours and mostly *Phyllostachys*. For orange-yellow right the way up the cane, with a series of green vertical stripes get *P. aureosulcata* 'Spectabilis'. Its minimum ground space is 60 sq cm (2 sq ft). Second, for groundcover, there is 90cm (3ft) high *Sasa veitchii*, and 30cm (1ft) high *Pleioblastus pygmaeus* which you can even mow. They will cover 1 acre (0.4 hectares). And third are clump formers like *Fargesia* which grow 3.7m (12ft) high and have small leaves with densely packed thinner stems.

Cultivation Bamboos are generally very long lived. Some species flower annually, but most of the species in cultivation may never flower outside of their habitats. The vast majority of cultivated bamboos are native to Asian countries. Apart from producing edible shoots, they have an enormous range of applications in building and furniture making. Bamboos are also used as garden stakes, and are split for making blinds and many woven products. The bamboo especially valued for split-cane fishing rods is the Tonkin bamboo, *Arundinaria amabilis*, but this is rarely cultivated as an ornamental.

BAMBOO AT A GLANCE

Excellent exotic plants to enliven the garden, adding shape and rich colours. Most hardy to -15°C (5°F).

		RECOMMENDED VARIETIES
JAN	/	*Fargesia murieliae*
FEB	/	*F. murieliae* 'Simba'
MAR	/	*F. nitida*
APR	divide 🖐	*Phyllostachys aurea*
MAY	repotting 🖐	*P. aureosulcata* 'Aureocalis'
JUN	restrict clump 🖐	*P. a.* 'Spectabilis'
JULY	restrict clump 🖐	*P. bambusoides* 'Allgold'
AUG	restrict clump 🖐	*P. nigra*
SEPT	/	*P. viridiglaucescens*
OCT	/	
NOV	/	
DEC	/	

KNOWN AS FISHPOLE OR GOLDEN BAMBOO, Phyllostachys aurea, *has large pendulous trusses of fine foliage. It makes a magnificent feature in a large garden where it can spread over a wide area to create a truly jungle-like atmosphere.*

Varieties The elegant black bamboo (*Phyllostachys nigra*), which grows 3–5m (10–15ft) high, makes a beautiful feature for a courtyard or terrace if grown in a large, decorative terracotta or glazed ceramic pot. Golden bamboo (*P. aurea*), also known as the fishpole bamboo, grows somewhat taller, with pretty canes becoming golden yellow in the sun and highlighting its green and gold foliage. The tender Buddha's belly (*Bambusa ventricosa*) is most often grown in a container with little water; this stresses the plant, keeping it to perhaps 1.8m (6ft) in height and forcing the base to swell and flare out, which produces the form that gives the plant its common name. Other excellent varieties include the bright orange-yellow, moderately invasive *Phyllostachys bambusoides* 'Allgold' which grows 4.5m (15ft) high. *P. vivax* 'Aureocaulis' has a superb yellow stem with striking random green stripes and panels. It grows about 7.5m (25ft) high. And *P. aureosulcata* 'Aureocalis'. has a burnt yellowy-orange colour that briefly turns red in the sun and grows 3.7m (12ft) high. For a tunnel of canes for children to run through grow the tall thin bendy Fargesia. And for a gentle thin screen, say one cane every 23cm (9in), buy *Phyllostachys aurea*, green, stiff and upright. Pruning gives that see-through effect.

CONDITIONS

Aspect Bamboos grow in full sun or partial shade.
Site They tolerate quite poor soil, but it must be well drained. Soils enriched with organic matter produce better foliage and growth.

GROWING METHOD

Propagation All bamboos can be grown by division. You will need a mattock or axe to divide some of the larger growers. Running types are easily grown from sections of the rhizome that contain a node. Both methods are best carried out in late winter to spring.

Feeding Unless soil is very poor, feeding is not necessary for ground-grown plants. Container-grown plants need either liquid fertiliser applied monthly through the growing season, pelletted poultry manure in spring and summer, or slow-release fertiliser applied in the spring.

Problems Bamboos are generally problem free, and a healthy plant that is well grown should look after itself. If a bamboo spreads too much (and you must check that you buy the right kind for your garden), slice off new stems poking up through the soil in the summer. This also opens up views through the clump.

FLOWERING

Season Note that the leaf development is completely unlike that of most other plants. The oldest canes in a clump are actually the thinnest and shortest. The new young ones are increasingly thicker and taller. They kind of rev up getting bigger and bigger. And the leaves and branches on the newest canes appear increasingly higher up. By the time the canes are 2.5cm (1in) thick the first leaves can be over head high.

FATSIA JAPONICA
Japanese aralia

IF YOU NEED A TALL SHRUB with big evergreen leaves for a slightly shady corner, try Fatsia Japonica. *It always catches the eye, and flowers in the autumn. To thrive, all it needs is protection from fierce winds.*

FEATURES

Sun

Partial Shade

An essential ingredient for the exotic garden, Japanese aralia, as it is sometimes called, is an extremely well known, underrated evergreen shrub. It produces hand-like leaves divided into fingers, 30cm (1ft) long, and grows about 3m (10ft) high. The display is enhanced in the autumn when creamy white flowers open. If the plant becomes too tangled and big, it is easily cut down to about 45cm (1½ft), and quickly regrows. If growing it as an architectural plant, you can prune it cutting away unwanted branches to give a particular shape. It is a particularly useful plant because it tolerates city pollution, and shady corners. There are three forms, 'Aurea', 'Marginata' and 'Variegata' which are variegated, but note they are all half-hardy. 'Moseri' is slightly smaller with larger leaves.

FATSIA AT A GLANCE

F. japonica is a big-leaved evergreen with autumn flowers which is ideal for slightly shady corners. Hardy to -5°C (23°F).

		COMPANION PLANTS
JAN	/	
FEB	/	Ceanothus
MAR	sow	Euphorbia
APR	/	Ficus
MAY	transplant	Hedera
JUN	/	*Paulownia tomentosa*
JULY	/	*Pseudopanax crassifolius*
AUG	/	Rosmarinus
SEPT	flowering	Vitis
OCT	flowering	
NOV	/	
DEC	/	

CONDITIONS

Aspect It likes both full sun and light shade, but the variegated kind needs a much higher proportion of shade than sun. Protection against cold, ripping winds is essential. This is particularly important for varieties with variegated foliage.

Site It will thrive in any typical garden which avoids extreme soil conditions. Water well in hot dry summers to counter evaporation from the leaves. Give the soil a mulch of well-rotted manure in the spring. This will help it to retain moisture during dry periods later on in the year.

GROWING METHOD

Propagation Cuttings of new growth in the first part of summer yield the best results. They should quickly root. Alternatively, sow seed in the spring or autumn.

Feeding A light summer feed is all that this plant requires. If it is fed too abundantly, fatsia becomes congested with elongated, soft new growth and leaves.

Problems Pests and diseases pose few problems, otherwise the main setbacks only occur when the plant is flayed by cold winds which ruin the leaves and cause die-back. Growing it against a wall is the best solution.

FLOWERING

Season The flowers only appear in the autumn. They are decorative not beautiful, but are perfectly good for cut flower displays.

FESTUCA GLAUCA
Blue Fescue

THE FINE, HAIR-LIKE FOLIAGE *of blue fescue, which is becoming increasingly popular for its natural unfussy look.*

A DENSE, WEED-PROOF EDGING *can be made by planting clumps of blue fescue not more than 25cm (10in) apart.*

FEATURES

Sun

Partial Shade

This dense, tufty grass is ideal for edging, groundcover or for filling pockets in a rockery, or used as a contrast among vertical plants. It must be thickly planted in pots for the best effect. A mature clump is usually less than 25cm (10in) high and about 20cm (8in) across. Many of the cultivars are shorter, with denser, more compact foliage, but 'Azurit' grows to 30cm (1ft). The fine foliage of the species is a distinct blue-green while cultivars range from dull or steely blue to olive-green. Many cultivars were raised in Germany and may be sold under their German or English names. 'Blaufuchs' ('Blue Fox') grows to 15cm and is a good, intense blue; 'Blauglut' ('Blue Ember') is a striking silver-blue; and 'Seeigel' ('Sea Urchin') has hair-fine green to blue-grey leaves.

FESTUCA AT A GLANCE

F. glauca is a superb perennial evergreen grass with blue-green leaves and summer flowers. Hardy to -15°C (5°F).

		RECOMMENDED VARIETIES
JAN	/	*Festuca amethystina*
FEB	/	*F. eskia*
MAR	sow	*F gautlieri*
APR	divide	*F. glauca*
MAY	divide	*F. g.* 'Blaufuchs'
JUN	flowering	*F. g.* 'Blauglut'
JULY	flowering	*F. g.* 'Elijah Blue'
AUG	/	*F. valesiaca* 'Silbersee'
SEPT	/	
OCT	/	
NOV	/	
DEC	/	

CONDITIONS

Aspect For best colour, this grass should be grown in full sun. If you can create a dry, Mediterranean- type garden area, this would be the most appropriate setting. The spiky, bluish leaves stand out particularly well when they are set off by a pale coloured gravel background. *Festuca glauca* can also be used as a 'dot' plant on a patio as it looks very striking when planted in gaps in the paving.

Site Any well-drained soil will suit this grass.

GROWING METHOD

Propagation Divide clumps every 2–3 years to maintain the plant's appearance and increase your stock. This is best done in spring or autumn. To maintain colour, division is the only viable method of propagation.

Feeding This grass tolerates very poor soil and should not need extra feeding.

Problems Regular removal of dead leaves and clippings in spring and summer helps to maintain good growth and colour. Plants should recover naturally when the weather cools. The centres of clumps may die out, particularly in warm, humid conditions.

FLOWERING

Season Flower spikes appear in the summer. They vary in colour and may be dense or sparse. Dense flower spikes, usually blue-green in colour, appear in summer and stand above the foliage. A few of the cultivars are sterile and produce no flowers at all.

FOENICULUM VULGARE
Bronze Fennel

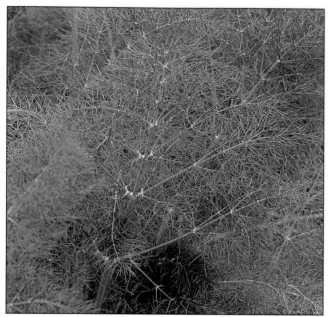

THE SMOKY-BROWN *feathery leaves of bronze fennel are carried on very fine stems. New growth in early summer is rapid and vigorous.*

SOFT, BILLOWING PLUMES *of bronze fennel reflect a paler tone of the burgundy shrub growing beside it.*

FEATURES

Sun

Bronze fennel is simply an ornamental form of common fennel. It is grown either in herb gardens or perennial borders for its wonderful purple-tinged bronze foliage, which gives the effect of plumes of smoke or a dark mist. Its fine, feathery foliage combined with its unusual colour make it unique and always a focal point in a garden. As it may grow to almost 2m (6½ft), it must be planted towards the back of a border or in the centre of a bed encircled by other lower growers. Like common fennel, it bears pretty, flat heads of small yellow flowers in mid- to late summer. It does not form the swollen stem base of finocchio or Florence fennel (*Foeniculum vulgare* var. *dulce*), which is used as a vegetable.

FENNEL AT A GLANCE

F. vulgare is a tall, good looking perennial herb which can also be a border feature. Excellent flavour. Hardy to -15°C (5°F).

		COMPANION PLANTS
JAN	/	
FEB	/	Basil
MAR	sow	Bay
APR	sow	Borage
MAY	transplant	Coriander
JUN	/	Mint
JULY	flowering	Parsley
AUG	flowering	Rosemary
SEPT	/	Rocket
OCT	/	Sunflower
NOV	/	
DEC	/	

CONDITIONS

Aspect   This plant prefers an open, sunny position where it will maintain good foliage colour.

Site   Although bronze fennel can be grown in any type of well-drained soil, the quality will be much higher if the soil is enriched with organic matter before planting. Note that the more prolifically the fennel puts on new growth the better both visually and in the kitchen. Handfuls of the leaves add a rich nutty flavour when roasted with a chicken. They completely lose their aniseed flavour.

GROWING METHOD

Propagation   Bronze fennel is best grown from seed which is sown in the spring. It is easily raised and presents few problems.

Feeding   Fertilising is not necessary, but on very poor soils you could apply some pelletted poultry manure or complete plant food in spring.

Problems   This is considered a tough, trouble-free plant.

FLOWERING

Season   Flowers are produced in mid- to late summer. These mature to form the aniseed-flavoured seeds used in cooking and some herbal remedies. All types of fennel produce large quantities of seed after the summer flowers fade. Unless you want a lot of self-sown plants, you should cut off the spent flower heads before the seeds set and mature. Newly formed seeds are pale green but mature seeds are creamy beige.

GUNNERA MANICATA

Gunnera

THE 'IT' PLANT FOR A BOG GARDEN *is* Gunnera Manicata. *It makes a tremendous show in the summer, with gigantic thick leathery leaves, thick stems, and magnificent flower spikes. If you can grow it on a bank giving views underneath, even better.*

FEATURES

Sun

Partial Shade

This is not a plant for small gardens. Growing to 2.5m (8½ft) high, clumps grow 3–4m (10–13ft) wide. The huge rhubarb-like leaves can be well over 1m (3ft) in diameter, and are supported by long, stout hairy stems. This is a magnificent feature plant from Africa, Australasia, and South America. It needs a damp or wet garden area beside a pond or stream. In summer it produces a dramatic tall spike of greenish flowers, often completely concealed by the foliage, but this plant is grown for the impact of its giant, architectural foliage. It is herbaceous, dying right back to the ground in winter. This is not a difficult plant to grow in the right conditions, but it must be carefully sited. It needs space to grow, and gardeners need space to stand back and admire it.

GUNNERA AT A GLANCE

G. manicata is one of the largest, most spectacular perennials with huge leaves and a spectacular flower spike. Hardy to -5°C (23°F)

		RECOMMENDED VARIETIES
JAN	/	*Gunnera arenaria*
FEB	/	*G. flavida*
MAR	transplant	*G. hamiltonii*
APR	divide	*G. magellanica*
MAY	divide	*G. manicata*
JUN	/	*G. prorepens*
JULY	flowering	*G. tinctoria*
AUG	/	
SEPT	sow	
OCT	/	
NOV	/	
DEC	/	

CONDITIONS

Aspect   Grows both in semi-shade and sun in cool, damp areas.

Site   Likes a deep, rich, moist soil. Dig plenty of organic matter into the ground before planting. Avoid free-draining ground.

GROWING METHOD

Propagation   Divide small clumps in the spring, replanting them no less than 2m (6½ft) apart. Cuttings can be taken from new growth, too. Pot them up and nurture them until they are well rooted. Plants can be raised from seed, but this is slow and difficult. Keep the new plants moist throughout spring and summer. Water well in dry periods to counter evaporation through the big leaves.

Feeding   Apply pelleted poultry manure as new growth commences in the spring to give a boost. Add a fresh mulch of rotted manure at the same time.

Problems   No specific pest or disease problems are known for gunnera.

FLOWERING

Season   Long dramatic spikes of greenish flowers are produced in early summer.

Fruits   The inflorescence is followed by fleshy red-green fruits, which can be used in cut flower displays.

AFTER FLOWERING

Requirements   Cut back brown leaves in autumn. Protect crown with layers of straw.

HEDERA
Ivy

IVIES ARE HUGELY UNDERRATED, and have all kinds of talents. They can climb up stout old trees, cover and insulate sheds, be grown up poles giving striking green verticals, trained as tall lollipops, and even used as hedges. There is a superb range of leaf colours.

FEATURES

Sun

Partial Shade

Ivies are excellent multi-purpose plants. Though there are only about 10 species, you can buy nearly 300 cultivars with a wide range of leaf size, from the tiny *Hedera helix* 'Spetchley', which grows 15–20cm (6–8in) high with a leaf the size of a fingernail to giants like the *H. colchica* with hand-sized leaves. There is an ivy for most situations, for covering old sheds under massive dense growth to creating extensive groundcover. Silvery *H. hibernica* 'Maculata' thrives in the shade, and others can be used for topiary. Train a vigorous, small-leaved kind through a 3-D frame. Ivy is also good for wildlife, the flowers attracting butterflies. Best of all ivy offers a range of hues and variegations, some brandishing big yellow or cream markings.

HEDERA AT A GLANCE

Indispensable climber which can provide an evergreen 'wall', be trained as topiary or used as groundcover. Hardy to -15°C (5°F).

		RECOMMENDED VARIETIES
JAN	/	*Hedera canariensis*
FEB	/	'Gloire de Marengo'
MAR	/	*H. colchica*
APR	/	*H. c.* 'Dentata'
MAY	/	*H. c.* 'Sulphur Heart'
JUN	/	*H. helix* 'Goldheart'
JULY	/	*H. h.* 'Green Ripple'
AUG	/	*H. h.* 'Spetchley'
SEPT	flowering ❀	*F. hibernica*
OCT	flowering ❀	
NOV	flowering ❀	
DEC	/	

CONDITIONS

Aspect Ivies, especially the variegated kinds, generally like good light, but some green-leaved plants grow successfully in the shade.

Site There is an ivy for most situations, excluding the wet and the dry, but as general rule provide moist, free-draining soil. Climbers need a solid structure, like a fence, a wall, or a trellis to climb over.

GROWING METHOD

Propagation Cuttings taken from the summer's growth yield the best results. They can be stuck in the soil, and should give a 90 per cent success rate, or they can be potted up and nurtured in the usual way.

Feeding Outdoor ivies do not need any feeding, but pot-grown kinds will need a summer feed to boost new growth. They should also be repotted with new compost each spring.

Problems Ivies are largely problem free, and once established can be left to look after themselves.

FLOWERING

Season The ivy's insignificant flowers appear in the autumn on mature plants. They are followed by small, round berries which provide a valuable source of winter food for wild birds.

Walls Ivy climbs by means of sticky pads which firmly clamp onto any surface. Although the pads do not have penetrative power, ivy will worsen the condition of mortar-weak walls. It should not be allowed onto roofs where it can get under and dislodge the tiles.

HELICHRYSUM PETIOLARE
Helichrysum

THE NEAT, VELVETY LEAVES of Helichrysum *'Limelight' lift a shaded corner of the garden; as its sharp colour is so outstanding.*

PLANTED IN A RAISED BED, 'Limelight' cascades over a wall. It also makes a pretty container plant if allowed to trail.

FEATURES

Sun

Partial Shade

Although it is a flowering plant, helichrysum is almost always grown for its foliage alone. It has clusters of small off-white, daisy-like flowers that add nothing to the decorative effect of the plant and are best removed when buds appear. A shrub-like perennial, helichrysum forms a mounded shape, but in some situations it has a tendency to sprawl or trail. In wild gardens, it will grow to about 1.2m (4ft) high and up to 2m (6½ft) wide, but it is easily kept to size by regular pruning. The foliage looks and feels felty as it is covered in a mat of dense, woolly hairs. In the species, the leaves are silvery grey, but there are a number of cultivars of varying foliage colour.

HELICHRYSUM AT A GLANCE

H. petiolare is a bright, lime green evergreen which is ideal for underplanting taller topiarised shapes. Half-hardy to 0°C (32°F)

		RECOMMENDED VARIETIES
JAN	/	*Helichrysum arwae*
FEB	/	*H. italicum*
MAR	/	*H. orientale*
APR	sow	*H. petiolare* 'Roundabout'
MAY	divide	*H. p.* 'Variegatum'
JUN	flowering ✿	'Schweffellicht'
JULY	flowering ✿	*H. splendidum*
AUG	flowering ✿	*H. stoechas*
SEPT	flowering ✿	
OCT	/	
NOV	/	
DEC	/	

Varieties A favourite cultivar is *Helichrysum petiolare* 'Limelight', which has outstanding, bright lime-green leaves. Both this and the species can be used to great effect to lighten a shaded area, either in the ground or as a container plant. 'Variegatum' is another excellent form. It is very similar but has greyish leaves with a marked cream variegation. 'Roundabout' is a miniature version growing 15cm (6in) high, with a spread of 30cm (1ft).

CONDITIONS

Aspect It does well in light shade or with morning sun and afternoon shade.

Site The soil must be fast draining, but should also contain some organic matter.

GROWING METHOD

Propagation Easily grown from tip or semi-ripe cuttings taken from spring to autumn.

Feeding Feeding is generally unnecessary, but a little slow-release fertiliser can be applied in spring.

Problems Poor drainage and overwatering are this plant's greatest enemies.

FLOWERING

Season Rounded heads of off-white daisy flowers appear in late summer or autumn. If you want to collect the seed, these heads can be left to mature and set seed, but they do not enhance the plant's appearance.

HOSTA
Plantain lily

THERE'S ALWAYS ROOM for at least one hosta. They can be grown to provide highly attractive ground cover, or feature plants, and the latter are best highlighted when grown in ornamental pots. New cultivars are constantly coming on to the market, often with striking patterned, coloured leaves.

FEATURES

Sun

Partial
Shade

Also known as the plantain lily, this herbaceous perennial is grown for its attractive, decorative foliage. The latter can be tiny or up to 45cm (1½ft) long. There are scores of excellent cultivars with leaf colour ranging from light to dark green, and from chartreuse to bluish. Many are variegated. Leaf texture also varies, and includes the smooth, shiny, matt, powdery, puckered and corrugated. Hostas excel at forming big bold clumps which keep down the weeds, but until they emerge in the spring weeding is vital. They look best when planted near water features, providing cover for slug-eating frogs, multiplying in the shade of trees, or individually highlighted in a pot with gravel on top of the soil. A good plant can become quite special when given this treatment.

HOSTA AT A GLANCE

A mainly clump-forming perennial from the Far East. Grow in courtyard pots or the border. Hardy to -18°C (0°F)

JAN	/	RECOMMENDED VARIETIES
FEB	/	*Hosta* 'Aureomarginata'
MAR	sow	'Blue Angel'
APR	divide	*H. fortunei aureomarginata*
MAY	transplant	'Francee'
JUN	flowering	'Krossa Regal'
JULY	flowering	'Royal Standard'
AUG	flowering	'Sagae'
SEPT	/	'Shade Fanfare'
OCT	/	*H. ventricosa*
NOV	/	*H. venusta*
DEC	/	

CONDITIONS

Aspect Most hostas can grow in full sun if they are well watered, but they really thrive in shade or dappled light. Note that blue-leaved forms can turn green with too much or too little shade, and that yellow-leaved kinds do best in direct sun in the early morning or late afternoon.

Site Provide rich, moisture-retentive soil. Dig large amounts of decayed manure or compost into the ground well before planting and mulch regularly afterwards.

GROWING METHOD

Propagation The quickest method is dividing the fleshy rhizomes in early spring. This is best done every four to five years.

Feeding Apply pelletted poultry manure in the spring.

Problems Slugs and snails can be a major problem, savaging the shapely leaves. When the latter are as good as the grey-blue 'Hadspen Blue', for example, they pose a major problem. Keep a regular lookout. Either deter with slug pellets or sharp sand around the stems.

FLOWERING

Season The flowers appear in the summer, the colours ranging from white to purple. They are held high above the foliage, and while those of *Hosta plantaginea* var. *japonica* or *grandiflora* are both white and lightly scented, the chief attraction of most hostas is their superb foliage; it can be oval, heart-shaped, rounded or pointed. Visit a specialist nursery when buying.

IMPERATA CYLINDRICA
Japanese Blood Grass

THE NEW GREEN GROWTH of this plant rapidly turns bright scarlet and deepens in colour as autumn approaches.

THE SLIM, UPRIGHT STEMS of Japanese blood grass are almost dwarfed by the heavy, sword-like leaves of iris.

FEATURES

Sun

Partial Shade

Only one variety of this grass is common in cultivation and that is *Imperata cylindrica* 'Rubra', also called 'Red Baron'. Known as Japanese blood grass in Europe and North America, it is an upright grower with slender leaves. It is a fairly slow-growing grass that makes a fine addition to a mixed border, where its form and colour provide pleasing contrast. It is also grown massed in containers. Growing to about 40cm (16in) high, the leaves emerge as mid-green and quickly become deep scarlet almost to the base. By autumn, the colours have become an even deeper red, which fades to a pinky brown as the plant becomes dormant. Since autumn colour is mainly seen in trees, this brilliant red is a real bonus and the grass deserves to be more popular.

IMPERATA AT A GLANCE

Japanese blood grass with its smart red tinge is an excellent plant, good for growing round ponds. Hardy to -5°C (23°F)

		COMPANION PLANTS
JAN	/	Convallaria
FEB	/	Eryngium
MAR	/	Iris
APR	divide	Leucanthemum
MAY	divide	Pennisetum
JUN	divide	Pulmonaria
JULY	/	Salvia
AUG	flowering	*Stachys byzantina*
SEPT	flowering	Verbascum
OCT	/	
NOV	/	
DEC	/	

CONDITIONS

Aspect It can be grown in full sun or partial shade. The main danger of growing it in the shade is that its colour will not develop its wonderful red hue, and its effect will be lost.

Site It grows best in slightly moisture-retentive soils rich in organic matter, but heavy clay soils that stay wet for long periods will cause plants to struggle, resulting in poor growth. Such soils are best tackled by digging in copious quantities of horticultural sand and grit, with some well-rotted compost, at a ratio of three to one in severe cases.

GROWING METHOD

Propagation Divide clumps of this grass in spring creating new plants to create extra cover.

Feeding If soil has been well enriched with organic matter, fertilising is generally unnecessary. Mulching in spring with manure or compost would be beneficial.

Problems No specific pest or disease problems are known. If plants lose their red colour and start to revert entirely to green, remove these sections at once. If not removed, they may spread wildly.

FLOWERING

Season This variety or cultivar does not generally produce flowers. In Australia it has a weedy relative known as blady grass that does seed prolifically and is a serious problem in warm regions, but it is not a problem in the cooler climate of northern Europe.

LIRIOPE MUSCARI
Liriope or *Lily Turf*

IF YOU *only grow one kind of* Liriope muscari, *choose the variegated form with its distinctive, fresh green and white foliage.*

ATTRACTIVE CLUMPS *of* Liriope *'Munroe White' accent a row of stepping stones sited in bark mulch.*

FEATURES

Partial
Shade

Shade

This is an easy-care foliage plant which is suitable for use in the garden as a groundcover or edging plant. Although it is herbaceous, dying down in the winter, liriope is also used as a container plant for seasonal effect. Because it dies back in winter, the new season's foliage is always fresh, bright and attractive. Growing 30cm (1ft) in height, the species has very dark green, narrow, strappy leaves, but the variegated forms are extremely popular and probably more widely grown. These variegated forms can be striped yellow and green, or cream and green. Sometimes also known as lilyturf, liriope may be confused with mondo grass, but is actually quite different. Liriope has deep violet-coloured flowers, while those of mondo grass are white.

LIRIOPE AT A GLANCE

L. muscari is a highly attractive perennial grown for its foliage, especially when variegated, and autumn flowers. Hardy to -18°C (0°F)

JAN	/	
FEB	/	RECOMMENDED VARIETIES
MAR	sow	*Liriope muscari* 'Big Blue'
APR	divide	*L. m.* 'Gold Banded'
MAY	transplant	*L. m.* 'Majestic'
JUN	/	*L. m.* 'Monroe White'
JULY	/	
AUG	/	COMPANION PLANTS
SEPT	flowering	Dicentra
OCT	flowering	Dryopteris
NOV	flowering	*Euphorbia robbiae*
DEC	/	Polypodium
		Ribes

CONDITIONS

Aspect   Liriope does not need full sun, instead preferring light or dappled shade. It also prefers slightly sheltered areas, away from cold winds.

Site   It can be grown in almost any soil, but thrives in a well-drained soil that has been enriched with manure or compost.

GROWING METHOD

Propagation   Lift and divide the clumps in spring and replant the single divisions at 10cm (4in) intervals. This is particularly useful when you need extra plants to encircle an island bed, for example.

Feeding   Pelleted poultry manure or complete plant food can be applied in spring.

Problems   No specific pest or disease problems are known to trouble this plant. However, slugs and snails can be a major nuisance. Keep a regular lookout at nights, and use slug pellets or traps if necessary.

FLOWERING

Season   Deep violet-coloured flowers appear on this plant right through the autumn. The blooms are long lasting in the garden, but do not last well as cut flowers. Cut off the spent flower stems once the flowers have dropped, and cut back the foliage as it dies back in late autumn.

Berries   Small black berries sometimes set after the flowers fade. If the berries mature and self seed, there is a good chance that the new seedlings will have plain green foliage.

LOMANDRA
Mat Rush

THE INFLORESCENCE *or flowering head of the mat rush is an attractive feature in bud, flower or seed.*

PLANTED IN A RAISED BED *to screen a fence, mat rush has a wide spread. Sea lavender and daisies fill the foreground.*

FEATURES

Sun

Partial Shade

Although there are many attractive species of *Lomandra* only one or two are common in cultivation. *L. longifolia*, the spiny-headed mat rush, is an evergreen with long, strappy leaves forming tufts or tussocks up to 1m (3ft) high and sometimes twice as wide. Spiny bracts that protrude beneath the flower clusters give the plant its common name. *L. glauca*, pale mat rush, is much shorter growing about 20cm (8in) high. It is rarely sold but is a very good plant. Mat rushes are used extensively in parks in Australia, both for toughness and ease of maintenance, but they make excellent garden plants. As low screens, bordering a path or as groundcovers, they can be used as mass plantings or as single accents. They are also easy to grow in pots.

LOMANDRA AT A GLANCE

Rarely grown but valuable Australian perennials with distinctive foliage and slightly scented flowers. Hardy to -5°C (23°F)

		COMPANION PLANTS
JAN	/	Convallaria
FEB	/	Echinops
MAR	transplant	Eryngium
APR	divide	Polygonatum
MAY	/	Pulmonaria
JUN	flowering	Sedum
JULY	flowering	Solidago
AUG	flowering	*Stachys byzantina*
SEPT	sow	
OCT	/	
NOV	/	
DEC	/	

CONDITIONS

Aspect Mat rush can be grown in full sun or in semi-shade. In hot climates, some shade is desirable. Plants grown in shade will be a deeper green.

Site This plant can be grown in almost any type of well-drained soil. It is remarkably non-fussy and easy to grow.

GROWING METHOD

Propagation Mat rush can be grown easily from fresh seed which should be sown as soon as it comes away readily from the flower spike. Clumps of this plant can also be divided. This is best done either in the spring, as full growth is about to begin, or in the autumn when the ground is still warm, giving the new sections time to get established before the winter.

Feeding It is not generally necessary to fertilise these plants as they are adapted to soils with a low nutrient content.

Problems These plants are generally trouble-free. Once established they require no attention. In cold regions pot up and keep under glass through the winter.

FLOWERING

Season Flowers in the summer. After the tiny flowers fall, the spiky seed heads can be dried and used in arrangements. Although the small, cream-coloured flowers are short lived, the clusters of rounded, yellow fruit capsules carried in sprays along the tops of the flowering spike remain decorative for a long time.

MAGNOLIA
Magnolia grandiflora

IF THERE'S A TOP 10 for the best plants to grow, Magnolia grandiflora *has to be on it. Against a warm sheltering wall it makes a fantastically tall, striking evergreen that is quite a star. But even better, it provides big white flowers with a gorgeous scent. The tree with everything.*

FEATURES

Sun

The best of a terrific genus, *Magnolia grandiflora*, sometimes called bull bay, is an evergreen tree that needs a high, warm sheltering wall to grow up. It can reach 30m (100ft) high in the wild, in south-east North America, but is more usually seen at about 12m (40ft) high in north European gardens where it is quite slow growing. It has large, shiny, dark green leaves about 20cm (8in) long and, from late summer to autumn bears fantastic creamy white flowers which are nearly 30cm (1ft) across. The scent is one of the strongest and fruitiest in the garden. Specialist nurseries offer dozens of excellent cultivars, including 'Exmouth', 'Goliath', and 'Victoria', which is one of the hardiest. 'Samuel Sommer' can produce flowers which are 45cm (1½ft) across.

MAGNOLIA AT A GLANCE

M. grandiflora is the most impressive tree you can grow, with rich evergreen foliage and stupendous flowers. Hardy to -5°C (23°F)

		RECOMMENDED VARIETIES
JAN	/	*Magnolia denudata*
FEB	/	M. 'Galaxy'
MAR	/	*M. grandiflora* 'Exmouth'
APR	transplant	*M. g.* 'Goliath'
MAY	/	*M.* x *loebneri* 'Leonard Messel'
JUN	/	*M.* x *soulangeana*
JULY	flowering	'Rustica Rubra'
AUG	flowering	*M. stellata*
SEPT	flowering	*M. wilsonii*
OCT	sow	
NOV	/	
DEC	/	

CONDITIONS

Aspect Provide full sun in a sheltered position which gives protection against cold winds.
Site The soil should be moist, well-drained and quite fertile. Plants will tolerate dryness much better once they are established. For the first few years make sure that they are well watered in hot dry summers.

GROWING METHOD

Propagation Take cuttings of the current year's growth in mid-summer and propagate in a 50–50 mix of seed-raising compost. Be patient as rooting is very slow. The small roots do not appear until the second month. Alternatively, raise from seed collected in the autumn. Remove the seeds from the pod and then remove the outer orange-red seed coating by soaking them for two to three days. Thereafter keep the seeds damp in a seed-raising mix.
Feeding *Magnolia grandiflora* will benefit from an annual mulch of well-rotted horse manure. Any more feeding can be counter productive as it will force the production of soft growth rather than flowers.
Problems This is largely a trouble-free plant, but keep a look out for red spider mites during very hot weather, though they never really become a major nuisance in a glasshouse. In rural areas protect against deer and rabbits by putting a tree guard around the stem.

FLOWERING

Season The superb white scented flowers appear from late summer through to the autumn.

MELIANTHUS MAJOR
Honey bush

THE HONEY BUSH is one of the most attractive, architectural plants for the garden. But note it is quite tender.

FEATURES

Sun

This very striking evergreen plant with its unusual blue-green foliage really stands out. It is grown as a feature in a mixed border or as a focal point in an annual or perennial display In a large garden it could be repeat planted to tie together various arrangements. The honey bush can grow up to 2m (6½ft) high, and it can spread by suckers forming a large clump if left undivided. The dark mahogany-red flowers contain copious quantities of nectar, attracting bees. Although native to South Africa, and initially tender here, after two years the base becomes woody and it can survive outside if given frost protection in mild areas. It can also be grown in a large pot.

MELIANTHUS AT A GLANCE

M. major is a slightly tender, southern African plant with striking foliage. It is damaged below -5°C (23°F).

		COMPANION PLANTS
JAN	/	Agave
FEB	/	Canna
MAR	sow	Choisya
APR	divide	Cordyline
MAY	/	*Hosta* 'Krossa Regal'
JUN	flowering ✿	Philadelphus
JULY	flowering ✿	Pinus
AUG	flowering ✿	Pseudopanax
SEPT	/	Salvia
OCT	/	Yucca
NOV	/	
DEC	/	

CONDITIONS

Aspect   Needs full sun, thrives on warm walls.
Site   The soil must be well drained but it need not be especially rich; in fact over-rich soils will produce good foliage effects but poor flowering. However, the outstanding architectural foliage is the main reason for growing this striking plant.

GROWING METHOD

Propagation   Grow from seed sown in the spring, or by dividing suckers on an existing plant, also in the spring. Plant at least 1m (3ft) apart. Give a deep watering every week or two in dry spells during the growing season.
Feeding   Apply complete plant food in the spring.
Problems   Red spider mites may strike. Use an appropriate insecticide.

FLOWERING

Season   Dark crimson flowers may appear in late summer or earlier on long stems which survived the winter.
Cutting   Flowers are probably best left on the plant as they do not smell particularly pleasant.

AFTER FLOWERING

Requirements Cut off the spent flower stems unless you are collecting ripe seed. Protect the base and roots with straw or bracken against frost. The older and woodier the plant, the better its chance of survival during the winter.

MISCANTHUS SINENSIS 'VARIEGATUS'
Miscanthus

SOFT, PALE GREEN AND WHITE growth make this grass easy to place in any colour scheme.

A SPREADING MOUND of miscanthus makes a good backdrop for smaller-growing annuals and perennials.

FEATURES

Sun

It has been cultivated in gardens since early this century and is also known as variegated Japanese silver grass. It forms a large, loose clump 1.8m (6ft) high and over 1m (3ft) wide. The pretty foliage bleaches to an overall beige-cream as winter approaches. This grass can be used to great effect in a mixed border, providing a total contrast in form to any other type of perennial. Its pale colour can also be utilised to contrast with dark green or burgundy-coloured shrubs. It makes an effective screen or windbreak and is also shown to great advantage when planted beside a pool. The latest trend in planting grasses like this involves growing them in flowing clumps, much as they would appear in the wild, with paths meandering between them. There are many excellent forms (see opposite).

MISCANTHUS AT A GLANCE

M. sinensis 'Variegatus' is a high quality perennial with variegated foliage and superb panicles. Hardy to -15°C (5°F)

JAN	/	RECOMMENDED VARIETIES
FEB	/	*Miscanthus floridulus*
MAR	sow ✍	*M. sacchariflorus*
APR	divide ✍	*M. sinensis*
MAY	transplant ✍	*M. s.* 'Ferne Osten'
JUN	/	*M. s.* 'Flamingo'
JULY	/	*M. s.* 'Gracillimus'
AUG	flowering ❀	*M. s.* 'Kleine Fontane'
SEPT	flowering ❀	*M. s.* 'Silberfeder'
OCT	/	*M. s.* 'Zebrinus'
NOV	/	
DEC	/	

CONDITIONS

Aspect   This plant is best grown in full sun in most regions, however, its delicate foliage may burn a little in the summer if the temperatures are very high.

Site   This plant prefers a moisture-retentive soil heavily enriched with organic matter. It often looks good when highlighted by plenty of gravel.

GROWING METHOD

Propagation   Mature clumps of miscanthus can be lifted and divided in the spring. This may require considerable effort as the roots are tough. After root division, cut the top growth down to a height of about 10cm (4in). Dividing a mature plant in this way can yield a rewarding quantity of vigorous young plants.

Feeding   The application of pelleted poultry manure and a generous mulch of decayed manure or compost should result in the best growth.

Problems   No specific pest or disease problems are known to trouble this plant.

FLOWERING

Season   The tall plumes of creamy beige to pink, silky flowers are held high above the foliage in late summer to early autumn. Cut them off as they become tattered, or allow them to be frosted for prolonged interest. If the flower heads are to be used for indoor decoration, they must be cut before the plumes become loose and fluffy. For flowers on shorter 1.2m (4ft) high stems grow 'Morning Light'.

MISCANTHUS S. 'ZEBRINUS'
Zebra Grass

YELLOW-GOLD BANDS *on* Miscanthus sinensis *'Zebrinus'*
become more evident as the weather warms up in June.

A LARGE MOUND of zebra grass features beside a gateway. Cut it
back hard each year so that the growth always looks fresh.

FEATURES

Sun

An excellent specimen plant, zebra grass also
makes a fine border or screening plant. Like
many other grasses, it is most effective planted
alongside a water feature where its reflection
multiplies its decorative effect. Growing from
1–2m (3–6½ft) high, its foliage arches
gracefully, soon forming a clump that will
spread to 1m (3ft) or so. It is distinguished by
its bright green leaves banded transversely in
gold. Gold banding does not appear until the
weather is consistently warm in early summer.
In cool climates, zebra grass browns off with
the first frosts, but even in warm areas it will
partially brown off during winter. It is best to
cut zebra grass back to the ground once it
starts to look tatty so that the new spring
growth will be bright and fresh.

MISCANTHUS AT A GLANCE

M. sinensis 'Zebrinus' is a high quality grass grown for its horizontal
yellow bands on the 1.2m (4ft) high leaves. Hardy to -15°C (5°F)

		RECOMMENDED VARIETIES
JAN	/	*Miscanthus floridulus*
FEB	/	*M. sacchariflorus*
MAR	/	*M. sinensis*
APR	sow 🖐	*M. s.* 'Ferne Osten'
MAY	divide 🖐	*M. s.* 'Flamingo'
JUN	transplant 🖐	*M. s.* 'Graziella'
JULY	/	*M. s.* 'Kleine Silberspinne'
AUG	flowering ❀	*M. s.* 'Variegatus'
SEPT	flowering ❀	*M. s.* 'Yakushima Dwarf'
OCT	/	*M. s.* 'Zebrinus'
NOV	/	
DEC	/	

Varieties   A similar cultivar, *Miscanthus sinensis* var.
strictus, known as porcupine grass in the
United States, has gold-banded foliage, but
its habit is fairly stiff and upright.

CONDITIONS

Aspect   This grass should be grown in an open and
sunny position. It thrives and looks best in
the light.

Site   Tolerant of most soils, zebra grass will grow
best in well-drained soils which have been
enriched with organic matter.

GROWING METHOD

Propagation   The best way to propagate, giving instant new
plants, is to divide an established clump in the
spring. Since the roots are tough it can be
quite hard digging them up, let alone dividing
clumps. It may require two people and two
forks. Each new section should have its own
root system.

Feeding   On poor soils apply pelleted poultry manure
as growth begins in spring. A spring mulch
around the plant also helps.

Problems   This plant is generally trouble-free.

FLOWERING

Season   In late summer or autumn, tall plumes of
coppery-pink flowers rise 30–60cm (1–2ft)
above the foliage. They can be picked and
dried for indoor use before they become fluffy,
or left to decorate the garden. Leave the stems
over winter to add extra interest.

OPHIOPOGON
Ophiopogon

THE PERENNIAL WHITE *flowers of mondo grass make a fine contrast with the dark leaves.*

IMPENETRABLE BY WEEDS, *a dense edging of mondo grass is virtually maintenance free.*

FEATURES

Shade

Partial
Shade

Ophiopogon japonicus, is the perfect edging plant, with dense, dark green growth to about 25cm (10in) high. It makes a thick groundcover for shaded areas and can be container-grown. It grows in clumps, spreading by running stems (stolons). A dwarf form growing only about 7.5cm (3in) high can be used for the same purposes. This is somewhat slower growing than the species. Long lived and needing little maintenance beyond an occasional thinning out, *O. japonicus* makes for easy-care gardening. Commonly used in Victorian gardens, it has again become increasingly popular in recent years. Although called grasses, these plants are actually related to lilies and do not belong to the grass family.

OPHIOPOGON AT A GLANCE

Exceptional grass-like perennials, the near black-leaved kinds now highly popular. Hardy to -15°C (5°F)

		RECOMMENDED VARIETIES
JAN	/	*Ophiopogon jaburan*
FEB	/	*O. j.* 'Vittatus'
MAR	transplant	*O. j.* 'White Dragon'
APR	sow	*O. japonicus*
MAY	divide	*O. j.* 'Kyoto Dwarf
JUN	/	*O. j.* 'Silver Dragon'
JULY	flowering	*O. planiscapus*
AUG	flowering	*O. p.* 'Nigrescens'
SEPT	sow	
OCT	/	
NOV	/	
DEC	/	

Varieties For a startling effect, try the almost-black form of *O. planiscapus* 'Nigrescens', which is often called 'Black Dragon' or 'Arabitus'. Rarely growing more than 20cm (8in) in height, it has to be planted in a good mass or its impact will be lost.

CONDITIONS

Aspect It grows extremely well in both full sun and partial shade. The dark-leaved varieties really stand out in bright light, or when grown in a bed which has been liberally covered with gravel or small pebbles.

Site Ophiopogon grows best in well-drained soils enriched with organic matter, although plants will tolerate poor soil.

GROWING METHOD

Propagation Lift and divide clumps in the spring. Each division must have its own roots and shoots. Since mass plantings of *O. planiscapus* 'Nigrescens' are particularly effective, it is far cheaper to keep dividing existing plants than to keep buying new ones.

Feeding Fertilising is not essential, but you can apply some complete plant food in spring or mulch around plants with manure or compost.

Problems No specific problems are known.

FLOWERING

Season Flower colour ranges from white to pale lilac. The plant usually flowers in summer.

Fruits Flowers are followed by blue, berry-like fruits.

PARTHENOCISSUS
Virginia creeper

If you want to cover a big wall with a big creeper, and get outstanding autumn colour, then go for a Virginia creeper. The most vigorous can easily grow 18m (60ft), and the end-of-season show of bright reds, purples and yellows, is spectacular.

FEATURES

Sun

The genus offers some of the very best climbers for rich autumn colour. The leaf colours range from dark purple at one extreme to flame red at the other. The 10 species climb using tiny tendrils with suckers on the end which firmly lock onto any surface. The creeper needs to be chosen with care. *Parthenocissus tricuspidata*, better known as Boston ivy, can grow 20m (70ft) high. It has 20cm (8in) long leaves that flare up in the autumn. Excellent forms include 'Lowii' with crinkled foliage. *P. quinquefolia*, Virginia creeper, with leaves half the size, grows 15m (50ft), and for a shorter creeper choose *P. henryana* which grows 10m (30ft) high; both turn bright red. The growth will not hurt a sound wall, but should be kept well away from roof tiles.

PARTHENOCISSUS AT A GLANCE

Powerful climbers which can cover the side of a house giving fantastic autumn leaf colours. Hardy to -15°C (5°F)

		RECOMMENDED VARIETIES
JAN	/	*Parthenocissus henryana*
FEB	/	*P. himalayana* var. *rubrifolia*
MAR	/	*P. quinquefolia*
APR	/	*P. tricuspidata*
MAY	transplant	*P. t.* 'Beverly Brook'
JUN	/	*P. t.* 'Green Spring'
JULY	flowering	*P. t.* 'Lowii'
AUG	flowering	*P. t.* 'Robusta'
SEPT	sow	*P. t.* 'Veitchii'
OCT	/	
NOV	/	
DEC	/	

CONDITIONS

Aspect   Grows in most positions, including walls facing north and east. The slightly tender *P. henryana* needs the protection of a wall where it will turn a brighter autumn colour.

Site   Most soils, avoiding extremes of wet or dryness, are fine. A rich soil which has had well-rotted compost dug in before planting will give the plant a big boost.

GROWING METHOD

Propagation   The best and quickest results are from early summer cuttings, or those taken in mid-summer. Pot up and they will soon develop good root systems. Seed can be sown in the autumn.

Feeding   These remarkably tough and resilient plants need no further pampering. With poor soil you can add an all-purpose spring fertiliser, and a spring mulch to help retain moisture.

Problems   Virginia creepers are completely trouble free, and only cause trouble if allowed to romp over too small a building, snaking between roof tiles and dislodging them. A better alternative, which few people do, is to let them grow up tall trees with the stems dangling out of the top, flying the amazingly colourful autumn foliage.

FLOWERING

Season   The creepers do actually flower, producing small insignificant greenish flowers which are followed by small blue or black berries, especially during hot dry summers. The berries are not to be confused with small grapes. They cause stomach upsets if eaten.

PENNISETUM
Pennisetum

SOFT, SILKY PINK plumes on the feathertop Pennisetum villosum *will gradually mature to almost purple.*

IN AUTUMN, the flower spikes on fountain grass have often faded, but still retain a decorative appearance.

FEATURES

Sun

The species name means feather bristle, from the Latin *penna* (feather) and *seta* (bristle). There are about 80 species throughout the tropics and temperate areas, flowering from mid-summer to autumn. As tall growing grasses, they make valuable additions to the garden. They look good mass-planted at the back of borders, as mini windbreaks or as lawn specimens. Their tolerance of wind and exposure makes them ideal for coastal gardens, and they can be planted to give a softening effect on hard landscaping. They provide stunning effects in both autumn and winter. Most fountain grasses become dormant in cool to cold winters, but in California and Australia some species self-seed prolifically and become serious aggressive weeds.

PENNISETUM AT A GLANCE

Superb range of perennial grasses from the tiny to 1.5m (5ft) high, with wonderful foliage and flowers. Hardy to -5°C (23°F)

		RECOMMENDED VARIETIES
JAN	/	*Pennisetum alopecuroides*
FEB	/	*P. a.* 'Hameln'
MAR	sow	*P. a.* 'Paul's Giant'
APR	divide	*P. a. viridescens*
MAY	/	*P. macrourum*
JUN	/	*P. orientale*
JULY	flowering	*P. setaceum*
AUG	flowering	*P. villosum*
SEPT	divide	
OCT	/	
NOV	/	
DEC	/	

Varieties

Pennisetum alopecuroides is a handsome, clump-forming grass growing to around 1.2m (4ft) high. Its stiff, foxtail flowers may be cream to pink or tan, maturing to reddish brown. Its cultivar 'Hameln' is a compact grower 50cm (20in) high. *P. villosum*, also known as feathertop, forms a loose clump of very narrow, green leaves growing to about 60cm (2ft) high. The cultivar of *P. setaceum*, known as 'Rubrum', is very popular as an accent plant and does not seed like the species.

CONDITIONS

Aspect Best grown in an open sunny spot, these plants are very tolerant of wind—in fact they look best when the stems are being swayed by the wind.

Site It can be grown in any well-drained soil.

GROWING METHOD

Propagation Divide fountain grass in the spring or autumn, which will instantly yield several new plants. Each one should have a piece of root with some top growth. Alternatively, sow new plants from seed as the weather warms up in spring.

Feeding Feeding is generally not needed, but some pelletted poultry manure or complete fertiliser may be applied in spring.

Problems No specific pests or diseases are known to trouble this plant.

FLOWERING

Season These grasses flower in summer or autumn. Remove flower heads to avoid seed setting.

PHALARIS ARUNDINACEA
Ribbon Grass

THIS VERY VIGOROUS GRASS is known as gardener's garters. It must be allowed a large space in the garden as it spreads rapidly.

IN EARLY SUMMER, ribbon grass starts to flower. This pale green and white grass is perfect in this meadow garden.

FEATURES

Partial Shade

Although this running grass has a tendency to be over vigorous, it is worth growing for the effect of its fine white and green striped foliage. This grass is an old favourite in northern hemisphere gardens where it is known as gardener's garters. Growing to about 1m (3ft) high, this most adaptable plant can be used as groundcover, as an accent planting in borders or simply as a feature on its own. The fine-striped foliage makes a good foil for other heavier-leaved plants, and is used both in fresh and dried flower arrangements. Foliage bleaches to a pale brown when frosted, but can be left in the garden for its winter effect. If the foliage is dull or floppy by mid-summer, cut it back to within 15cm (6in) of the ground for a fresh flush of new growth.

PHALARIS AT A GLANCE

P. arundinacea var. *picta* is a highly undervalued spreading grass which can grow in a wide range of conditions. Hardy to -15°C (5°F)

		COMPANION PLANTS
JAN	/	*Ajuga reptans*
FEB	/	Centaurea
MAR	/	*Digitalis purpurea*
APR	/	Geranium
MAY	divide 🖑	Grasses
JUN	flowering ❀	*Monarda fistulosa*
JULY	flowering ❀	*Polemonium caeruleum*
AUG	/	Silene
SEPT	divide 🖑	Solidago
OCT	/	Trifolium
NOV	/	
DEC	/	

CONDITIONS

Aspect It grows best in filtered sunlight or with morning sun and afternoon shade.

Site This plant is adaptable to almost any soil either wet or dry. Soils enriched with organic matter will give best results. It can also be grown in very shallow water. However, beware of growing ribbon grass, or gardener's garters as it is sometimes known, in a border because it will quickly spread over large areas, ruining your planting plan and dominating less vigorous plants. It is best grown as groundcover, perhaps by the side of a stream, or at the end of a garden where it turns into a wild section. Whatever its site, this plant needs to be grown with great care, so that it does not run out of control.

GROWING METHOD

Propagation Ribbon grass is grown from divisions of clumps taken during late winter to early spring or autumn. They should guarantee plenty of growth and spread.

Feeding Fertilising is generally not necessary for these plants unless the soil is extremely poor.

Problems No specific pest or disease problems are known. Any stems that revert to plain green should be cut off as soon as they appear.

FLOWERING

Season Plumes of pale green, flowering spikes appear in summer. These age to a pale beige colour and are popular for use in decorative arrangements either fresh or dried.

PHILODENDRON
Philodendron

THE HEART-SHAPED LEAVES *of this* Philodendron *have strongly marked veins. The leaf reverse is dark crimson.*

IN TROPICAL GARDENS, Philodendron selloum *often climbs high into trees. Elsewhere, it usually has a large, shrub-like form.*

FEATURES

Shade

Partial Shade

Grown for the architectural effect of their large shapely leaves, philodendrons are easy-care plants for shady sites. They need either a space in the border or a large pot, and since they quickly grow quite tall you will not be able to move them outside for the summer. They bring a strong sense of the exotic, coming from South American rainforests, particularly in Brazil and Columbia. Their large leaves can reach 60cm (2ft) long in the case of *P. angustisectum*, and 1m (3ft) with *P. bipinnatifidum* and *P. melanochrysum*. The second of this trio has the most distinctive leaves because they are like hands with about 20 fingers. The most frequently grown kind is *P. scandens* (a good houseplant) which has glossy green heart-shaped foliage pointing

down. These plants are probably best seen in botanical glasshouses because they are quite demanding to keep. Besides all-year round summer heat, they need plenty of humidity, and misting at least twice a day.

CONDITIONS

Aspect   It grows best in shade or dappled sunlight. Avoid growing exotic climbers in front which might block out the light.

Site   The soil or potting mix must drain well, but should also have a high organic content.

GROWING METHOD

Propagation   Can be grown from stem cuttings taken any time through the warmer months, or from seed if available. Sow seed in spring.

Feeding   Slow-release fertiliser or pelleted poultry manure can be applied throughout the growing season. Add a mulch, compost or manure in spring. They are quite hungry feeders, but overdoing it can result in an abundance of soft growth.

Problems   This plant is generally trouble-free, but keep an eye out for scale insects and red spider mite during the hottest months.

FLOWERING

Season   The flowers—produced intermittently—are of the arum lily type, with a green to purplish spathe (leaf-like bract) and a cream spadix (central column).

Fruits   Fruits containing seeds mature on the spadix.

PHILODENDRON AT A GLANCE

Exceptional conservatory shrubs and climbers grown for their marvellous leaves, providing evergreen cover. 15°C (59°F) min.

		COMPANION PLANTS
JAN	/	Anthurium
FEB	/	Calathea
MAR	sow	Caladium
APR	/	Dracaena
MAY	transplant	*Ficus benjamina*
JUN	/	Hibiscus
JULY	/	Jasminum
AUG	/	Mandevilla
SEPT	/	Passiflora
OCT	/	Peperomia
NOV	/	Tillandsia
DEC	/	Vriesea

PHORMIUM
Flax

STIFF, OVERLAPPING LEAVES of an unusual shade of blue grey make the cultivar 'Dancer' worth seeking out.

A BRONZE-LEAVED FORM of flax contrasts nicely with the deep green of a formally clipped hedge.

FEATURES

Sun

Although long used by the Maori people for fibre to be made into clothing, ropes and nets, this New Zealand plant is not botanically related to the linen flax, *Linum usitatissimum*. New Zealand flax leaves were also used whole to weave into mats and baskets. There are only two species of *Phormium*, both of which are native to New Zealand and Norfolk Island, but the extensive hybridising of the past 20 years has resulted in many colourful and exciting cultivars. Flax has always been popular as an accent plant in borders, a lawn specimen or for general form and foliage contrast.

PHORMIUM AT A GLANCE	
Excellent evergreen perennials famed for their colourful, stiff sword-like foliage. Hardy to -5°C (23°F)	
JAN /	RECOMMENDED VARIETIES
FEB /	*Phormium cookianum*
MAR sow	P. c. 'Cream Delight'
APR divide	P. c. 'Duet'
MAY divide	P. c. 'Tricolor'
JUN /	P. c. 'Sundowner'
JULY flowering	P. tenax 'Nanum Purpureum'
AUG flowering	P. t. Purpureum Group
SEPT divide	P. t. 'Variegatum'
OCT /	
NOV /	
DEC /	

Species

The two species are *P. cookianum*, which has broad strappy leaves of slightly weeping habit and forms a clump about 2m (6½ft) high and wide, and *P. tenax*, a stiff, upright plant with sword-shaped foliage that grows to 4 m high and about 2m (6½ft) wide. Both these species have long been popular ornamental plants in the garden.

Cultivars

Cultivars of *P. tenax*, which have been available for many years, include 'Aurora', which has dull burgundy foliage, and 'Variegatum', with creamy yellow or white stripes. Cultivars of *P. cookianum* include 'Tricolor', which has leaves margined creamy yellow and red and was the first ornamental cultivar discovered in 1880. Today, there is a wonderful collection to choose from in terms of both colour and size, as many ornamental hybrids have been raised from both the original species. Cultivars are grouped roughly according to the dominant foliage colour, for example, bronze-leaved hybrids, yellow-leaved hybrids, and hybrids with red, orange or pink leaves. This last group has some glorious foliage colours in sunset shades. These plants include 'Dazzler', which grows to 60cm (2ft) and has narrow, bronze leaves striped bright red or pink in the centre; 'Maori Sunrise', which grows to 90cm with leaves striped apricot, pink and bronze; and 'Firebird', which grows to nearly 2m (6½ft) in height and has purple-bronze leaves with red margins. Flax leaves, especially the richly coloured types, are popular with florists and cultivars are grown to supply this market.

BRIGHT PINK MARGINS *on bronze-coloured foliage are a feature of several of the newer cultivars of flax.*

STIFF GREEN AND YELLOW FLAX *rises out of a bed of red salvia. The contrast in both colour and form is striking.*

CONDITIONS

Aspect   These plants need an open, sunny position to maintain their foliage colour.

Site   All types of flax require fairly well-drained soils, although *P. tenax* tolerates almost any soil, whether dry or marshy. Soils enriched with organic matter will give better growth rates and good-looking foliage. It is important not to plant too deeply as this may cause the plant crowns to rot.

GROWING METHOD

Propagation   Both the species *P. cookianum* and *P. tenax* can be raised from seed or by division of existing clumps in spring. The cultivars must be grown by division. When dividing the plants, take care not to damage the growing tip and the young shoots in the centre of clumps as the regrowth will start from here. Dividing clumps of flax can be very hard work as the strong roots are tenacious, but it should be done every 3–4 years. Dividing plants in this way will yield a regular supply of new ones. They can easily be used in the garden, in a Mediterranean section, to fringe a path or to encircle an island bed.

Feeding   Apply pelleted poultry manure or complete plant food in spring and again in mid-summer.

Problems   There are no specific pest or disease problems known to trouble this plant.

FLOWERING

Season   The flowers of *P. cookianum* are a yellow-green colour, while *P. tenax* has dull red flowers. Both plants are pollinated by honey-eaters in their native New Zealand and also in Australia. The flowers which appear each summer are a decorative feature of the species, but they add little to the effect of the coloured leaf forms. When choosing a plant you should remember this and make leaf shape and colour your top priority. In the case of a plant like 'Sundowner' the leaves can be quite eye-catching. The flowers are a secondary consideration.

HINT

Pruning   To maintain the colour of variegated cultivars, cut off and discard any fans of foliage that revert to plain green or bronze. Groom the plants regularly by removing old leaves from the outside of the fan, cutting as low as possible with a sharp knife or secateurs. This must also be done in late winter to spring as new growth starts to emerge.

PLEIOBLASTUS
Pygmy Bamboo

LIGHT, PRETTY FOLIAGE is a feature of all the dwarf bamboos. Pleioblastus auricomus is the species most often seen in gardens.

THIS NEAT AND LIGHT-COLOURED dwarf bamboo is confined by a root barrier on the garden side to check its spread.

FEATURES

Sun

Many of these bamboos were previously classified as *Arundinaria* species and originate in China and Japan. All are running types that can spread dramatically and they need a big space to grow in. You can try to control them by slicing off new shoots with a spade.

Use dwarf bamboos as border or edging plants or simply to contrast against heavy-textured, darker-leaved plants. Some of the variegated forms can be a real feature in the garden. The true dwarf bamboo, *Pleioblastus pygmaeus*, rarely grows more than 30cm (1ft) high and spreads about 1m (3ft). It has pretty, bright green foliage. It is a good groundcover in areas where its spread can be confined.

Varieties

P. auricomus has yellow foliage which is striped green, and it needs full sun to retain its colour. Cut back in the spring and it soon puts out masses of fresh new growth. The variation *chrysophyllus* has new foliage that is yellow with no striping, but some stripes may appear later. *P. chrysophyllus* is moderately vigorous with cream or white variegation.

CONDITIONS

Aspect
Most species prefer light shade, while others need plenty of sun.

Site
Soil should be well drained and enriched with plenty of compost or manure.

GROWING METHOD

Propagation
In spring, dig up a section and divide into smaller sections for replanting. Make sure that each section has a piece of root and some top growth. Division is by far the quickest method of increasing your stock, and one mature new plant can immediately provide four new smaller ones.

Feeding
During the growing season only, feed with blood and bone or pelletted poultry manure.

Problems
A trouble-free plant, but drought does cause leaf drop and waterlogged soil induces root rot.

FLOWERING

Season
Flowers occur infrequently and are unusual in cultivated plants.

PLEIOBLASTUS AT A GLANCE

Excellent mini bamboos giving a big display of massed thin leaves up to 35cm (14in) long. Hardy to -15°C (5°F)

		RECOMMENDED VARIETIES
JAN	/	*Chusquea culeou*
FEB	/	*Fargesia robusta*
MAR	/	*F. spathacea* 'Simba'
APR	divide	*Indocalamus tessellatus*
MAY	divide	*Phyllostachys*
JUN	divide	*Pleioblastus auricomus*
JULY	/	*Sasa kurilensis*
AUG	/	*Semiarundinaria fastuosa*
SEPT	/	
OCT	/	
NOV	/	
DEC	/	

RODGERSIA
Rodgersia

RODGERSIAS MAKE EXTREMELY ATTRACTIVE, eyecatching plants for damp gardens, where their foliage really stands out. You can further highlight them by setting them apart, and covering the adjacent ground with gravel or pebbles. R. podophylla *is a particularly excellent choice.*

FEATURES

Sun

Partial Shade

A six-species genus with particularly interesting foliage and flowers, ideal for the border or shady woodland garden. The three most commonly grown kinds are *R. aesculifolia*, *R. pinnata* and *R. podophylla*, the last two having handsome, bronze foliage. All form big, bold clumps in the right conditions. The first has crinkled leaves like those of a horse-chestnut, up to 25cm (10in) long, with tall panicles of creamy white flowers, and a height of 2m (6½ft). *R. pinnata* 'Superba', 1.2m (4ft), has purple-bronze foliage and white, pink or red flowers. And *R. podophylla*, 1.5m (5ft), with creamy green flowers, also has horse-chestnut type leaves, turning reddish in the autumn.

RODGERSIA AT A GLANCE

Tall, clump-forming perennials which add shape and structure to dampish gardens. Hardy to -18°C (0°F)

		RECOMMENDED VARIETIES
JAN	/	*Rodgersia aesculifolia*
FEB	/	*R. pinnata*
MAR	sow	*R. p.* 'Elegans'
APR	divide	*R. p.* 'Superba'
MAY	transplant	*R. podophylla*
JUN	/	*R. sambucifolia*
JULY	flowering	
AUG	flowering	
SEPT	/	
OCT	/	
NOV	/	
DEC	/	

CONDITIONS

Aspect All rodgersia, from the mountaineous Far East, like full sun or partial shade.

Site Grow in rich, damp ground.

GROWING METHOD

Propagation Either divide, which is the easiest method, or grow from seed in the spring, raising the plants in a cold frame. Water the new young plants well, and do not let them dry out in prolonged dry spells. They quickly wilt and lose energy, and their performance is badly affected.

Feeding Add plenty of well-rotted manure or compost to the soil. The shadier the conditions, the less rich the soil need be.

Problems Vine weevil grubs can demolish the roots of container-grown perennials. While slugs rarely attack the new emerging growth, when they do strike they can ruin a potentially impressive display including tall, astilbe-like flowers. Pick off any offenders, or treat with a chemical.

FLOWERING

Season Flowers appear in mid- and late summer, or in early summer in the case of *R. sambucifolia*.

Cutting Rodgersia make good cut flowers.

AFTER FLOWERING

Season Cut the spent stems to the ground when the plants have finished flowering and promptly remove them all from the site to avoid the risk of disease.

STIPA GIGANTEA
Giant feather grass

WITH BEAUTIFUL SILVERY stems once summer arrives, Stipa gigantea is the king of ornamental grasses.

FEATURES

Sun

The extremely popular *Stipa gigantea* is one of the very best ornamental grasses. It is also known as golden oats and Spanish oat grass and comes from Spain, Portugal and Morocco. It is the largest feather grass and grows about 2.4m (8ft) high in the summer. It is grown for its mound of green leaves and the dozens of elegant silvery stems topped all summer by spikelets which turn gold in the autumn. It is an excellent plant for filtering a view, and benefits from being in the open where it gets swayed by the wind and lit by the sun. By the end of autumn the stems are a biscuit-beige colour. Leave them until the following spring. They liven up the winter garden, especially when turned into stiff white frosty shapes.

STIPA AT A GLANCE

S. gigantea is an excellent flowering perennial grass with a big impact for nine months a year. Hardy to -15°C (5°F)

		COMPANION PLANTS
JAN	/	
FEB	/	Briza
MAR	sow	Calamagrostis
APR	divide	Deschampsia
MAY	/	*Melica macra*
JUN	/	Miscanthus
JULY	flowering	Panicum
AUG	flowering	Pennisetum
SEPT	flowering	*Stipa arundinacea*
OCT	/	*S. tenuissima*
NOV	/	
DEC	/	

CONDITIONS

Aspect
Grow in full light, particularly with a view to its being lit by the late afternoon autumn yellow sun; it really brings out its colour.

Site
Provide moderately fertile, free-draining soil. It is a remarkably tolerant plant, and thrives in most conditions, provided they are not too extreme, such as wet boggy ground. It suits Mediterranean-type gardens, offset by gravel.

GROWING METHOD

Propagation
By far the best way to increase your stock of plants is to divide them any time from mid-spring to early summer. Make sure that each section has a well-developed root system, and a supply of green leaves. The old plants can be very hard to dig up and split, and you well need an extra pair of hands to help. Alternatively grow from seed sown in the spring.

Feeding
A scattering of an all-purpose feed in the spring is generally sufficient, unless the soil is very poor in which case dig in plenty of compost to add nutrients and aid water retention.

Problems
Overwatering or poorly drained soils will rot and kill the *Stipa gigantea*. Otherwise a totally trouble-free plant, but do stop to pick dead leaves out of the base clump of foliage, and occasionally to comb it upwards.

FLOWERING

Season
Marvellous open panicles all summer, which benefit from being backlit by the sun so you can appreciate their delicate structure.

INDEX

Published by Merehurst Limited, 2000
Ferry House, 51–57 Lacy Road, Putney, London, SW15 1PR

Text copyright © Merehurst Limited
Photograph copyright © Murdoch Books (except those listed below)

ISBN 1 85391 838 5

A catalogue record of this book is available from the British Library.

COMMISSIONING EDITOR: Iain Macgregor
SERIES EDITOR: Graham Strong
TEXT: Richard Rosenthal
MANAGING EDITOR, CRAFT & GARDENING: Christine Eslick
EDITORS: Helena Attlee, Susin Chow, Diana Hill
DESIGNER: Michèle Lichtenberger
EDITORIAL AND DESIGN SERVICES: Prima Creative Services
SERIES DESIGN: Jackie Richards
ILLUSTRATOR: Sonya Naumov
PUBLISHING MANAGER: Fia Fornari
PRODUCTION MANAGER: Lucy Byrne
UK MARKETING & SALES DIRECTOR: Kathryn Harvey
INTERNATIONAL SALES DIRECTOR: Kevin Lagden
CEO: Robert Oerton
PUBLISHER: Catie Ziller
GROUP CEO/PUBLISHER: Anne Wilson

PHOTOGRAPHS
Lorna Rose (all unless specified otherwise); Geoffrey Burnie (56R, 69R); Garden Picture Library (12); Margaret Hanks (17R, 42R,);
Stirling Macoboy (32); Murdoch Books Picture Library (9, 14, 64, 87, 105, 83, 104);
Jo Whitworth (46, 51, 58, 81, 84L, 84R, 89, 90, 92, 107L, 108, 109).

FRONT COVER: *Rhipsalidopsis gaertneri*
TITLE PAGE: Barrel cactus coming into bloom